Kingdom Living for the Family

by

Frank and Ida Mae Hammond

KINGDOM LIVING FOR THE FAMILY
ISBN 0-089228-100-6
Copyright © 1985

Impact Books, Inc.
137 West Jefferson
Kirkwood, Missouri 63122

Cover Design: Mary Uhring

We Are Grateful

For Kathy Jobert and Joyce Wilbanks in typing and retyping the manuscript. Also for Jerry Low in editing the first draft, and for Phyllis Jennings for her professional proofreading skills in perfecting the final copy. These have all served in love, offering their time and talents as unto the Lord.

Introduction

In 1968 the Lord literally thrust my wife and me into the ministry of deliverance when we were in our twentieth year of pastoral work. Such ministry immediately plunged us into deep involvement with personal and family counseling. We found it impossible to minister deliverance effectively without corresponding counsel. Also, we found that counsel, apart from deliverance, was incomplete. Counsel and deliverance were discovered to be inseparable tools.

It also became apparent that in order for people to be set free from their bondages, root problems had to be solved. In most cases we discovered the roots went back to the formative stages of a person's life; early childhood and even the prenatal period. Family-related factors going back to when an individual was yet an embryo, an infant, or a child had opened the doors for evil spirits to enter and indwell.

Since so many problems could be traced back to early life, it became apparent that may doors to demonic activity could be closed through the strengthening of families. Therefore, there emerged, along with our emphasis upon deliverance, a corresponding emphasis upon the family.

Family life is a life of relationships. Until these relationships are healed and the family brought into the ways of God, there can be no unity, peace or love. The family will be unable to function spiritually, and the devil will attack each family member. Thus, there is established the priority of healing bruised and broken relationships among family members. The healing of relationships involves repentance of sin, changes in behavorial patterns, changes in attitudes and prejudices, discipline of life and deliverance from evil spirits.

The distinctive feature of this book on family relationships is its scripturally based counsel in correlation with the ministry of deliverance.*

*If the reader is unfamiliar with deliverance, he is referred to *Pigs In The Parlor*, a practical guide to deliverance ministry, by Frank and Ida Mae Hammond; Impact Books, 137 West Jefferson, Kirkwood, Missouri 63122.

TABLE OF CONTENTS

CHAPTER I

Kingdom Living — God's Family Plan

God has a wonderful plan for each family; to bring the family into Kindgom living. Do you realize what this means? "For the kingdom of God is. . . righteousness and peace and joy in the Holy Spirit"* (Romans 14:17). This verse describes the condition of all who enter into Kingdom living. Too many families have settled for much less than God has provided. Instead of righteousness, there is weeping, wailing and gnashing of teeth; instead of peace, there is turmoil, conflict and confusion; instead of joy, there is discontent, unhappiness and hurt.

Each family needs a vision of God's promises and provision. There must be hope. There must be an understanding of how to enter into Kingdom living. There must be an assumption of personal responsibility. There must be cooperation with God and with one another. There must be determination to possess what is rightfully one's own. Kingdom living is for those who are serious about the things of God. From the first of Christ's teachings on the Kingdom, there have been those determined to possess its prize:

> "And from the days of John the Baptist until now the ✓
> kingdom of heaven suffers violence, and violent men take
> it by force" (Matthew 11:12).

The Kingdom of God

The Kingdom of God is a government. It has authority;

*All references are from the *New American Standard Bible* unless otherwise indicated.

1

it has a King; it has spiritual law. To come into the Kingdom of God is to place one's self under the King by submitting to His government. God has ordained that His government embrace the family. He did not create the family and then leave it to its own devices to make its own way. The family is an extension of God's government in the world. Each family must be set in Divine order. Divine order for the family is outlined in I Corinthians 11:3:

(1) Christis the head of every man

(2) The man is the head of a woman

(3) God is the head of Christ

The truth, concerning Divine order for the family cannot be bypassed. It is essential to the well-being and functioning of the family. Just as it was necessary for Christ to acknowledge the headship of the Father, so must the man acknowledge the headship of Christ, and the woman acknowledge the headship of her husband. This is THE divinely established order for the family. It cannot be altered or set aside if one wishes to obtain the blessings of Kingdom living.

God's order for the family is given and enlarged upon in the book of Ephesians and is simply outlined:

(1) *The husband's headship:* "For the husband is the head of the wife, as Christ also is the head of the church, He Himself being the Savior of the body" (Ephesians 5:23).

(2) *The wife's submission:* "Wives, be subject to your own husbands, as to the Lord" (Ephesians 5:22).

(3) *The children's obedience and respect:* "Children, obey your parents in the Lord, for this is right. Honor your father and mother (which is the first commandment with a promise), That it may be well with you, and that you may live long on the earth" (Ephesians 6:1-2).

The first step for the family is to acknowledge itself as an extension of God's government, and purpose to fulfill its function as a part of God's Kingdom. The benefits of

Kingdom life are obtained as a by-product of Kingdom order and priority. As Jesus said, "But seek first His kingdom and His righteousness; and all these things shall be added to you" (Matthew 6:33).

Peace and joy are things added to those who make the Kingdom of God their priority. We desire the benefits, so we seek a place in the Kingdom where they are found. Jesus Christ becomes our King; we make Him Lord in all things; we become His subjects and do His pleasure. Now we are eligible for the blessings of Kingdom living. We can then expect to experience the blessings of joy and peace which are characteristics of the Kingdom of God and its King.

Within the Kingdom of God are all of the things we need. Even our material needs are supplied. Our needs for food, shelter and clothing become the responsibility of our King. He must assume responsibility for these provisions and "add" them to us. It delights the King to provide for us. But our needs are more than material. Peace is a legitimate need, and our King is the Prince of Peace. "There will be no end to the increase of His government or of peace" (Isaiah 9:7). Peace is inherent in the King; it comes to us through our relationship with Jesus, our King. Also notice that peace is in conjunction with His governing. As His government increases, peace increases. Whatever His government embraces, peace is the result. This applies to the family as well as to individuals and nations. On every level there is peace for those under the complete Lordship of Jesus Christ, the Prince of Peace.

The Kingdom Principle Illustrated

While He was ministering in Capernaum, a certain Roman centurion begged Jesus to heal his servant boy. In other words, this military captain wanted the benefits of Kingdom living. He wanted healing for someone under his headship. But there was a problem. This man was a gentile, a heathen outside the covenant of God. Such blessings

3

were only for God's children and heirs of promise. However, the centurion understood Kingdom principles better than do most of God's own children. He proceeded to submit himself totally to the authority of Jesus:

> "But the centurion answered and said, 'Lord, I am not worthy for You to come under my roof, but just say the word, and my servant will be healed. For I, too, am a man under authority, with soldiers under me; and I say to this one, "Go!" and he goes, and to another "Come!" and he comes, and to my slave, "Do this! and he does it' " (Matthew 8:8-9).

This man had faith to submit himself and his need to the King. Submission to authority requires trust in that authority's ability and love. Each husband and father must do what this centurion did: submit everything to Jesus. Thus, Christ becomes the head of man!

The centurion had authority himself, and his authority meant responsibility for those under him. Since he did not have the resources in himself to heal his servant, he submitted himself to the One who did. This is the pattern of Kingdom submission which God approves and honors. Husbands and fathers have grave responsibilities to provide for and protect those under them: responsibilities far too great for themselves alone. Such heads of families must, in faith, acknowledge the headship of Jesus.

By the husband/father's submission to the headship of Jesus, the family then has as its true head the One described through Isaiah as the "Wonderful Counselor, Mighty God, Eternal Father, Prince of Peace" (Isaiah 9:6b). The government of God now embraces that family.

Jesus marveled at this gentile's faith submission, and pointed out that those who appear least likely to receive Kingdom benefits may, in fact, be the first to obtain them. The Jews had better advantages, but were slower to respond.

There is no necessity for God's children to be outside His blessings. Yet, experience has proven time and time again that many Christian families are missing the benefits

4

of Kingdom living. The reason is plain: the head of the family has not recognized Jesus as Lord, and/or the wife and children have not recognized the headship of the husband/father. The consequences of such failure result in keeping the family outside the benefits of God's Kingdom. What is it like to be outside God's Kingdom?

> "But the sons of the kingdom shall be cast out into the outer darkness; in that place there shall be weeping and gnashing of teeth" (Matthew 8:12).

Notice, these people are called "sons of the Kingdom." They are heirs of God's Kingdom, but they are removed from its blessings. Through their lack of trust and obedience, they have become disqualified. They remain outside the lighted palace of the King.

There are conditions to receiving God's blessings. God has assured each family of a place in His Kingdom: a place of righteousness, peace and joy; but the conditions must be met. How genuinely does the family desire God's best? Enough to meet God's conditions? Enough to identify with His government through submission to His Lordship?

CHAPTER II

Warfare

Once we have accepted the challenge of getting ourselves and our families into Kingdom living, we must be prepared for war. There may be areas in the lives of each family member where Satan has been entrenched for years. He will not give up without a fight. Also, there is much new territory to claim; and Satan will contest us for each step along the way. It is comforting and reassuring to know that God has promised us victory. God has equipped us with every spiritual weapon and resource needed for the battle. As a believer, the same Spirit that raised Christ from the dead dwells in you. You are able to stand in God's strength and in the power of His might.

The family must understand spiritual warefare. It must learn to cast out devils and wrestle against the satanic principalities and powers of darkness and evil.

Get to the Roots

The purpose of the warfare is to remove from our families everything pertaining to the satanic kingdom, and to establish our families in the ways of God. We must begin by discovering all the inroads the enemy has made and learn to think "roots." That is, to ask God to enable us to see behind the surface problems we are facing. How and when did the enemy gain entrance?

Most persons who come to us for counseling and ministry are very conscious of their surface problems: the things that

6

are troubling them at the moment. As they relate their surface problems, we must seek God's wisdom in discerning the root problems. One must learn to examine his problems as he would examine a tree. When one first looks at a tree, he is most aware of its leaves. The leaves are the predominant feature of the tree. The leaves parallel surface problems. Closer examination reveals that each leaf is supported by a twig, each twig is supported by a small limb, each small limb is supported by a larger limb; and the larger limbs are supported by the trunk of the tree. In similar fashion, there is a demonic support system for every surface problem.

One of the most important facts that is to be learned in spiritual warfare is that demons are closely linked with one another. In the individual deliverance, we are not dealing with isolated and unrelated spririts, but we are dealing with a system of spirits. We will always find spirits linked together with other spirits. There is a "kingdom" of spirits within each person to whom we minister deliverance.

After we have traced the problem from the leaves to the trunk of the tree, we still have not uncovered that which gives life to the tree. There is a part of the tree that is hidden from view. The root system lies beneath the surface and must be dug up. We already know the roots are there, because we can see what they have produced. These roots must now be uncovered and destroyed.

Most of our initial attempts at deliverance merely dealt with leaves and small limbs. We could not understand why a person's problems kept coming back until we learned to deal with the root problems. We can remove leaves from a tree, but they will soon grow back. We can cut off limbs, but soon new limbs will appear. The only way to effectively destroy a tree is to destroy its roots.

Family problems have roots. Let me illustrate this from my own home. There was tension and conflict in our marriage over the handling of finances. It was like an underlying current of evil that continually disrupted our relationship. I felt that my wife was too sensitive over my handling of family finances and did not trust my judgment in financial decisions. On the other hand, she felt that she did not get enough consideration and had many needs that were never met. She felt condemned if she purchased something for herself, resentful if she was not allowed to purchase things for herself, and frustrated over how much say so she had in deciding family expenditures. Above all, she was fearful of my reaction to her financial requests.

The Lord convicted me of selfishness and of needing to be in control. I had to become honest and humble about my own faults. I had been brought up during the depression years. Money was scarce and a frequent source of discussion in the home. Every penny had to be accounted for. Things became all-important. Certain things were "mine," and my brothers could not touch them. I kept my personal belongings separate in dresser drawers and cigar boxes. My selfishness in the handling of family finances was rooted in childhood. It was true; I honestly did not give enough consideration to the things my wife needed.

I was also ruled by fear. I had never learned to trust God for the things I needed. In my family upbringing I was continually subjected to fear, worry and anxiety over the future and not having enough money to buy what was needed. I was suffering from financial insecurity. This insecurity caused me to exercise unnecessary control over the finances and thereby put pressure on my wife.

Now, selfishness, covetousness, fear, anxiety, worry and control are sins. Such sins open the door for evil spirits to enter. In order to be free I had to confess my sins, repent of my sins, ask my wife to forgive me, learn to trust God for my finances and cast out every demon spirit that compounded my problems. This was *my road* to freedom.

Ida Mae also had root problems to conquer. She was raised in semi-poverty in a family of six children. Her father was unable to finance her college education. His support was limited to five dollars which he gave her when she entered college. She had no money for personal items like

8

toothpaste, so she brushed her teeth with salt from the school dining hall. Most of her clothes were borrowed from classmates.

The constant financial pressures caused her to indulge in a fantasy that one day she would marry a rich husband who would buy her everything she needed. Instead, she married a poor preacher boy, and together they went off to seminary financed by the G.I. Bill and fifty dollars per month for pastoring a small country church.

Years later, after God began to prosper us, the financial pattern from early life still kept us bound and created conflict between us. There was a process through which God carried us as we became honest before Him and transparent with one another. The axe was laid to the root problems. Old habit patterns were changed, demons were expelled and financial conflicts were resolved.

Facing Spiritual Opposition

Anyone who is awake to the spiritual realm senses the spiritual opposition from Satan against his family. Satan knows that a family submitted to God's Divine order is a threat to his own kingdom. He has no access to such a family. Somehow, he must weaken and destroy the Divine order of the husband's headship, the wife's submission and the children's obedience. He will do everything he can to keep God's order from being established in the family, and to overthrow every situation where it is already established. This means that there must be warfare to establish and maintain the family in God's Kingdom.

The devil knows that the family is strategic in conquering anything else. He knows that no nation, community or church is stronger than the families that comprise it. If he can defeat the family, he can conquer the world. If he can defeat us at home, we are ineffective for God elsewhere. Satan will do everything within his bag of lies, deceptions, accusations and threats to keep family relationships from

9

being healed.

In too many instances the devil is responsible for stirring up strife in families and getting its members in conflict with one another while he goes unchallenged for his part in it. We must learn that ". . . our struggle is not against flesh and blood, but against the rulers, against the powers, against the world forces of this darkness, against the spiritual forces of wickedness in the heavenly places" (Ephesians 6:12). As long as the devil can keep us fighting and blaming one another, he escapes detection and confrontation. This does not take away from our dealing with problems in our flesh, but we must realize that few of our problems are flesh alone. Our problems are compounded by *demonic infestation*. The remedy for unruly flesh is mortification and discipline (See Colossians 3:5-10); the remedy for demonization is deliverance (See Matthew 8:16).

Deliverance

How does one know whether his problems are of the flesh or of demons? Suppose a husband gets angry occasionally, and in such times of anger, he lashes out at his wife and says things to hurt her. Does he need deliverance from a demon of anger, or does he need to discipline his flesh? Has his wife nagged him and caused him to explode? Is she the one who needs deliverance rather than the husband? Or, does each of them need both deliverance from demons and the discipline of their tongues?

There is something that few persons seem to understand unless they have been directly involved in deliverance ministry, and it was a surprise to me when I began to minister deliverance. I quickly became aware of how prevalent demons are and how readily they enter a person. Those who lack this comprehension are prone to judge deliverance ministers as "seeing a demon behind every bush." Truly, there is no shortage of evil spirits, and they enter wherever a door of opportunity is opened.

10

WRATH IS A WK OF THE
IDOLATRY FLESH
ALSO WORSHIP & EVIL OR WITCH-
CRAFT

In Ephesians 4:26-27 we are told, "Do not let the sun go down on your anger, and do not give the devil an opportunity." Letting the sun go down on your anger means going to bed without repenting of the sin of anger and without restoring relationship with the one with whom you became angry. By so doing you have opened the door of sin and left it open. An open sin door gives an opportunity for the devil to get in. It seems that most people are quick to wrath and slow to repentance. James 1:19-20 says, "But let everyone be quick to hear, slow to speak and slow to anger; for the anger of man does not achieve the righteousness of God." Anger is not a work of righteousness, but of sin. It calls for prompt repentance. Anger triggers the tongue and others are wounded. So, repentance must be forthcoming, broken relationships must be mended, discipline of emotions and tongue must be achieved; and demons must be cast out.

In Galatians 5:19-20, "wrath" is listed as one of the works of the flesh. Now, the listing of the works of the flesh also includes idolatry and witchcraft. These are readily identified as demonic works, so why are they listed as fleshly works? Because these sins have their origin in the flesh. Wherever there is sin (works of the flesh), demons will be attracted. It goes on to say in Galatians 6:8, "For the one who sows to his own flesh shall from the flesh; reap corruption . . . ." When a man sins, he is sowing to the flesh; and the harvest will be dead flesh (corruption). Do you know what is attracted to dead flesh? If there is a dead animal in the field, what will be attracted to it? Buzzards and other carrion-eating creatures that feed on dead flesh. Demons are like creatures that feed on dead flesh. This is what attracts them. Sin in one's life produces dead flesh, and demons begin to gather around.

What can be done when buzzards are feeding on a dead animal? If you drive off the buzzards, they will immediately return unless you remove the dead thing upon which they are feeding. The spiritual application is exactly the same. If one wants to get rid of and stay free from a "spiritual buzzard" (demon), he must clean up the dead flesh. He must

11

DEAD TO FLESH VS DEAD FLESH
(In Sin)

repent of his sin, receive God's forgiveness, and with the aid of the Holy Spirit discipline that area of his life so that he will not continue to sin.

> "Do you not know that when you present yourselves to someone as slaves for obedience, you are slaves of the *one whom* you obey, either of sin resulting in death, or of obedience resulting in righteousness?" (Romans 6:16).

Notice that yielding to sin is yielding to a "whom"; a personality. Satan is a personality, and sinning is yielding to him. Through sin he gains a legal right to our lives. The only way to keep him out is to stop sinning and by prompt repentance when sin does occur.

It was not long after I began ministering deliverance to others that I became aware of my own deliverance needs. On the whole, I have always been a rather amicable person, and I was proud that I was not like other men who gave way to anger and violence. Well, I did get angry once in a great while. I could remember five or six times in my life when I had become excessively angry. Surely, I thought, so few problems with anger would not indicate a demon of anger. Then I became angry one day toward my daughter who was a teenager at the time. The anger did not last long, but it was so intense that I lost control of my reason for a few minutes. I still did not think much about it until I did the same thing again about a week later. It frightened me to think that I could have injured my daughter in such a time or rage. Could such anger be demonic?

A few days later I had the opportunity to submit myself to another pastor who knew how to minister deliverance. He felt that my anger was demonic and proceeded to command the demon of anger to leave me. I was standing in front of this other minister and was taken by surprise when I suddenly fell to my hands and knees and began to growl like a bear. Then the demon of anger left me. That has been twelve years ago, and I have not once had another bout with uncontrollable anger.

When I sought the Lord as to how such an ugly demon of anger entered me, the Lord reminded me of the time when I became violently angry with one of my brothers. I was probably nine or ten years of age, and my brother was doing something to irritate me. I picked up a heavy metal toy and threw it at him. Fortunately, it missed, but it crashed into the door with such force that it left quite a dent in the door. What might it have done to his head? I then chased him out of the house. I had picked up a baseball bat and was trying to catch him to "clobber" him. He ran across the street right in front of a passing car and almost got hit by the car. The driver of the car slammed on the brakes and stopped just in time. This brought me back to my senses, and my anger cooled off. But that was how and when the demon of anger entered.

In like manner most persons have opened themselves to the invasion of evil spirits. Therefore, each member of the family should submit himself to the ministry of deliverance, and the family should begin to learn how to minister deliverance to one another. The conflicts between family members represent a "sniper fire" of indwelling demons in the lives of each of the members of the family. Demons in a wife are "sniper-firing" at the husband and vice versa, and demons in parents and children are "sniping" at one another. Such families live in continual peace-destroying strife. This is not Kingdom living for the Kingdom of God is peace. Such families need to get the devil kicked out and Jesus enthroned as Lord. Peace is available; it is just waiting to be appropriated.

Sometimes one member of the family is waiting for the others to get deliverance and get their acts straightened out. It is easy to think that all of our shortcomings are due to someone else's wrong behavior, and that when he behaves properly, then we will have no further problems. In other words, we think all of the changing needs to be done by others rather than by ourselves. A wrong *reaction* is as wrong as a wrong *action*. If a husband reacts wrongly to his wife's nagging, then he also has a problem. He is not Christlike if he gets angry, rails at her, buries resentment inside himself or storms out of the house. We cannot justify our sins because someone else has done wrong.

It is not unusual for families to be so spiritually divided that they cannot cooperate in getting their deliverances and working together toward the grand goal of getting the family into Kingdom living. Most often, it is the husband/father, the head of the family, that is unwilling to do his part. There is no getting around the fact that this attitude creates an unfortunate disadvantage to other family members who genuinely desire the full blessings of the Lord in their home. But that husband/father is still the head of his family in the sight of God, and must be respected as the head. There are things the other members of the family can do to better conditions in the home. (We will come to this later on.)

Let each member of the family make it his own priority to get his *own life* into the Kingdom. Let those family members who are open to deliverance get their deliverances and then discipline every area of spirit, soul and body. The fruit of that action will be the ability to "walk in the Spirit," no matter how others are behaving. Even if only one member of the family will be a consistent Christian example, it will have its influence upon the others.

> "For how do you know, O wife, whether you will save your husband? Or how do you know, O husband, whether you will save your wife?" (I Corinthians 7:16).

Family Curses

The roots of a family's problems can go back several generations in their ancestry. There can be family curses due to the sins of one's parents, grandparents, or great-grandparents. Some curses go back many generations. It is important to understand the principles governing curses. There are six facts to grasp:

14

1. "So a curse without cause does not alight" (Proverbs 26:2b). No one is under a sin curse except sin has opened the door for it. Wherever there is indication of a curse, we must begin to look for the cause. There is no effect of a curse except there be a cause for a curse.

2. Sin introduces the curse. Sin opens the door for a curse to enter. Genesis 3:14-19 gives the account of sin's introduction into human experience. Sin brought a curse upon each one involved: the serpent, the woman and the man.

    (1) And the Lord God said to the serpent,
    "Because you have done this,
    Cursed are you more than all cattle. . .
    On your belly shall you go,
    And dust shall you eat
    All the days of your life. . . ."

    (2) To the woman He said,
    "I will greatly multiply
    Your pain in childbirth,
    In pain shall you bring forth children;
    Yet your desire shall be for your husband,
    And he shall rule over you."

    (3) Then to Adam He said. . .
    "Cursed is the ground because of you;
    In toil you shall eat of it
    All the days of your life.
    "Both thorns and thistles shall grow for you;
    And you shall eat the plants of the field;
    By the sweat of your face
    You shall eat bread,
    Till you return to the ground. . . ."

    Not only did sin bring a curse upon those present at the time of sin, but also upon the descendants of Adam.

    "Therefore, just as through one man sin entered into

the world, and death through sin, and so death spread to all men, because all sinned. . . by the transgression of the one, death reigned through the one. . . through one transgression there resulted condemnation to all men. . . through the one man's disobedience the many were made sinners" (Romans 5:12, 17-19).

The people of the Old Testament days were very aware that the curse of a man's sins was passed down to his descendants. They had coined a proverb that said, "The fathers eat the sour grapes, but the children's teeth are set on edge" (Ezekiel 18:2).

In the ten commandments, God gave commandment not to make any graven images nor to bow down and serve them: ". . . for I, the Lord your God, am a jealous God, visiting the iniquity of the fathers on the children, on the third and the fourth generations of those who hate me" (Exodus 20:5).

3. The power of a curse is demonic. Wherever a curse is in operation, demons are operating. In Genesis 3:15, as soon as sin and its curse appeared, the serpent was given power to strike: ". . . And you shall bruise him on the heel."

King Saul is another example. He rebelled against what God told him to do, for God told him to go smite the Amalekites until they were utterly destroyed. But, he spared King Agag along with sheep and cattle. This sin brought God's curse upon Saul, and Saul became insane. His insanity was demonic.

"Now the spirit of the Lord departed from Saul, and an evil spirit from the Lord terrorized him" (I Samuel 16:14).

4. The law provides no remedy for the curse.

"For as many as are of the works of the law are under a curse; for it is written 'Cursed is everyone who does not abide by things written in the book of the law, to perform them' " (Galatians 3:10).

You will remember that David committed the sins of

16

adultery and murder. Even though he repented with a broken and a contrite heart, the curse was not removed from his family. It passed down to his children and grandchildren. Nathan, God's prophet, foretold the curse to fall on David's family.

"Now therefore, the sword shall never depart from your house, because you have despised Me and have taken the wife of Uriah the Hittite to be your wife. Thus says the Lord, 'Behold, I will raise up evil against you from your own household; I will even take your wives before your eyes, and give them to your companion, and he shall lie with your wives in broad daylight. . . ' " (II Samuel 12:10-11).

The curse that came upon David's family was of like nature to David's sins of adultery and murder. The Old Testament history records the sad story of sexual immorality and bloodshed that was set in motion in David's family.

5. In Christ we are redeemed from the curse of the law. We are not under the power of sin's curse any longer.

"Christ redeemed us from the curse of the Law, having become a curse for us — for it is written, 'Cursed is everyone who hangs on a tree' " (Galatians 3:13).

There is now a remedy for the curse of sin. No one need remain under generation curses. This precious promise was revealed many times and in many ways through the prophets of old. For example:

"In those days they shall not say again,'The fathers have eaten sour grapes, and the children's teeth are set on edge.' But everyone will die for his own iniquity; each man who eats the sour grapes, his teeth will be set on edge. Behold days are coming, declares the Lord, when I will make a new covenant with the house of Israel, and with the house of Judah" (Jeremiah 31:29-31).

We are under that new covenant. It is a covenant of grace. Its benefits are *not conditioned upon what we do, but upon what God, in Christ has done for us.* The sins of the father need no longer pass down to succeeding generations, neither need any person remain under the curse of sins committed by his ancestors.

6. The redemption must be appropriated. Christ's redemptive work was sufficient to save all of mankind, but not every one has benefited from the purchased redemption. Redemption is not automatic. "The gospel of Christ is the power of God unto salvation, to every one who believes" (Romans 1:16).

Eternal salvation is part of Christ's redemption. It is appropriated by those who put their faith in Him for salvation. Healing and deliverance from demons are also included in redemption.

"And when evening had come, they brought to Him many who were demon-possessed; and He cast out the spirits with a word, and healed all who were ill in order that what was spoken through Isaiah the prophet might be fulfilled, saying, 'He Himself took our infirmities, and carried away our diseases' " (Matthew 8:16-17).

Remember, the confession of sin is only the prelude to deliverance. Faith is important to deliverance, but one cannot "faith" a demon out. The way to get a demon out is to cast him out. That is, one does not merely *believe* God to remove the demon. God has given us authority over unclean spirits; *we must cast them out in His name.* His name is our authority. One must exercise faith to cast out a demon.

Examples of Family Curses

The reader would do well to take time now to read through Deuteronomy 27-28. He will find an extensive treatment of curses. There is a long listing of sins which bring curses, and then a long listing of the kinds of problems produced by curses: the causes and effects of curses. Then, in

18

the 30th chapter, the option is given of obedience and blessing, or disobedience and cursing. Who would hesitate over such a choice? Let us all say with Joshua, "As for me and my house we will serve the Lord" (Joshua 25:15b).

I have previously called attention to David's sins and the curses that remained upon his family. In this case, the curses were of the same nature as David's sin. Because of his immorality, there was a curse of immorality throughout his family. This is sometimes the pattern, but not always. The curse of sexual sin may be mental illness, disease or any number of things. Nevertheless, there are many cases of widespread sexual sins within families which have their roots in the family ancestry due to fornication, adultery, bestiality or incest on the part of parents, grandparents or great-grandparents.

In addition to the curses incurred by persons committing sexual sins and the resulting repercussions within their families, the victims of sexual sins are left with damaging scars within their personalities. Judging from the number of cases we uncover in personal counseling, I would estimate that as many as one fourth of the women to whom we minister have been victims of molestation, incest or rape.

It is no wonder that some women have developed a deep distrust, disrespect and hatred of men because of sexual abuses in childhood. These abuses of the female in childhood usually carry over to cause repercussions in marriage relationships. The wife may be frigid and unable to enjoy a normal relationship with her husband. The husband, in turn, becomes resentful, frustrated and sexually rejected. Since sexual compatibility is so important to unity and peace in the marriage relationship, the devil is able to damage or wreck the husband-wife relationship because of problems rooted in childhood experiences.

It is not only girls that are abused sexually, but also boys. A case in point is that of a man who came to us for deliverance from alcoholism. As we talked, it was learned that he had a very deep resentment toward the church and had quit attending any church. The root of his problem went back to childhood when he had had a Sunday school teacher who was homosexual. This teacher would lure him to his place of business at night and there molest the boy. The boy's mother, not suspecting the motives of the teacher encouraged her son to go with the man when he came by to pick him up. The young boy was too afraid to tell anyone what was happening to him. The guilt and confusion resulting from this abuse had produced a hatred of the church and its leaders and had driven the man to alcohol.

In addition to the list of incestuous curses found in Deuteronomy 27:20-22, there is an even more extensive list in Leviticus 18:6-17. Any sexual relations between persons of near kinship will bring a curse upon that family. God told His people, Israel, that such sins defile the land and are an abomination unto the Lord. It was because of such sins that the Canaanites were destroyed and Israel given their land for an inheritance. But, if Israel committed such sins, they would be driven from their inheritance as were the Canaanites.

A whole nation can come under a curse because of the widespread sins of *incest, adultery, homosexuality,* and *bestiality.* When we reflect upon the mushrooming of such sins throughout our own nation, we can begin to understand why an Elijah ministry which calls the nation to repentance will be the only thing sparing us from the wrath of God.

Illegitimate birth is another source of curse upon the family. The King James translation uses the word "bastard" to refer to a child conceived or born out of wedlock.

> "A bastard shall not enter into the congregation of the Lord; even to his tenth generation shall he not enter into the congregation of the Lord" (Deuteronomy 23:2).

Who knows whether there has been an illegitimate birth in his ancestral line as far back as ten generations? I make it a practice to routinely break all inherited curses from the person to whom I minister. Why not make the following

20

confession and prayer right now in the following way:

> "Lord, Jesus Christ, you are my Savior. You died on the cross for my sins and rose again from the dead. I now confess unto You all my sins and the sins of my ancestors. Every curse that would come upon me because of their sins is now broken. I break these curses off my family. I stand upon Your promise that You have redeemed me from the curse of the law. I command every evil spirit which has gained power in my life through ancestral sins to leave me right now in the Name of the Lord Jesus Christ."

It is being said through the news media today that some ethnic and racial groups in the United States now have over 50% of their children born illegitimately. Such groups have a curse upon them which is evidenced by the poverty and disease which besets them. Such problems can never be remedied by social reform any more than a band-aid can cure an infected wound.

Bestiality is yet another sexual sin which has brought generation curses into families, and in our observation has produced some of the most serious of curses. The scripture says, "Cursed is he who lies with any animal" (Deuteronomy 27:21).

One day I was asked by a pastor with whom I was ministering to go with him to a certain home where he said an unusual demonization was being manifested. There, I witnessed the most bizarre manifestations of a curse I had ever encountered. There were three adolescent children in that family, and all three of them were like animals in behavior. None of us could get near these children; they acted like frightened animals. They would leap about the room and across the furniture with the agility of monkeys. They would not use a bathroom, and the house reeked of the odors of urine and excrement. They were running in and out of the house the entire time we were there. I looked into the back yard and there was a children's swing-set upon which they would do their acrobatics, and they drank from a plastic wading pool by lapping water into their mouths with their hands. None of them could talk, but could only make squealing noises. What a pathetic sight! What could have caused such a condition in these children?

The father of the children was not there, but I was able to talk with the mother. I asked her if there had been any bestiality in the family. She shared with me that her husband was obsessed with bestiality and continued to practice it regularly. He had even persuaded his wife to lie carnally with dogs while he watched. These poor children were suffering in their bodies and lives the curse of their parent's sins.

In another instance, my wife and I were asked to minister to a man who was insane. He had not been able to work or to function as a husband and father for ten years. His wife and children were suffering in many ways from his insanity.

Ida Mae and I began to pray that the Lord would enable us to minister effectively to this man. How we longed to see him set free. At the same moment, the Holy Spirit gave both of us the same word of knowledge: This man had committed a sin which he had never confessed, and it had brought upon him the curse of insanity. The Holy Spirit was revealing to us that he must first confess this hidden sin in his life as the prerequisite for deliverance. When he was confronted with this fact, he dropped his head and refused to talk. We kept reminding him that he must talk to us about what he had done and that the Lord would forgive him of that sin when he repented and confessed it. Finally, he told us that as a young man he had had sexual relationships with farm animals. The devil had persuaded him that he had committed an unpardonable sin, and there was no need to seek God's forgiveness.

The guilt he was suffering was intolerable. His pastor had told us that this man could not read the Bible. When he had been asked to read from the Bible, he would read just a few words and then begin to rip the pages apart. The reason for this was that he now feared God's judgment and

BEFORE DEL

COULDN'T READ THE BIBLE

22

that the Scriptures reminded him of a hopeless sinfulness and God's punishment.

We were able to lead him in a prayer in which he confessed the sin of bestiality and accepted God's forgiveness. He also forgave and accepted himself. The curse of *bestiality* was broken, and the system of spirits which held him in bondage was cast out. A year later we received a beautiful letter of thanksgiving from this man and his wife. They testified of complete deliverance from insanity. The wife wrote, "I now have a new husband."

So, we learn from Deuteronomy 27:21 and Leviticus 18.23 that *bestiality* brings a curse. One of the effects of such a curse can be insanity: "The Lord will smite you with madness . . ." (Deuteronomy 28:28). Further, the father's sin would have passed the curse of insanity down to his children had not his sin been confessed and the curse broken.

Indeed, *sexual sins* and *perverseness* have brought many people and families under the power of demons, and the resulting curses have brought disease and mental illness, even as God has warned.

> "And the men also turned from natural relations with women and were set ablaze (burned out, consumed) with lust for one another, men committing shameful acts with men and suffering in their own bodies and personalities the inevitable consequences and penalty of their wrong doing and going astray, which was (their) fitting retribution" (Romans 1:27, Amplified).

Occultism is yet another source of curses upon families. *Occultism* is a form of *idolatry.* Through involvement in the occult, a person actually seeks knowledge, wisdom, guidance and power from sources other than God. We must remember that it is idolatry that is mentioned in the Ten Commandments as bringing a curse upon a person which will pass down to his third and fourth generations.

I have found and broken many curses upon people whose ancestors were worshippers of heathen deities, such as those

23

of African, American Indian and Oriental descent. Even in certain countries of western culture today, witchcraft and occultism are rampant. This is true of West Germany, England and even the United States. For these reasons, it is prudent to consider one's ancestral roots when breaking generation curses.

A few years ago I was ministering in a service where a young man, a deaf mute, was present. He was brought to the service by his mother who told us that her son was born totally deaf. The Holy Spirit gave my wife a word of knowledge that the young man's deafness was the result of his mother's involvement in fortune-telling. The mother confessed that she had been extensively involved in fortune-telling prior to her salvation. The mother was led to repent of the sin of fortune-telling, and to ask that the curse of occultism be broken off her and her son. When the demons of this curse left, the boy began to hear normally. Of course he could not talk because he had never heard speech and would need to learn to talk, but we played music over the church's sound system and he grinned and nodded his head to the beat of the music. The next day the mother called to verify that her son was indeed healed.

Ida Mae's family was also under an occult curse. Her father, although a devout Christian, was also a water-witcher. (Many Christians have ignorantly gotten involved in occult activities without any knowledge of the serious consequences.) The people of his rural community would call upon him when a new water well needed to be located. He would take a forked stick and walk across their property until the stick would bend toward the ground by supernatural power. This practice is a form of *divination* forbidden in Deuteronomy 18:10. It will bring a curse upon a man and his family. Ida Mae's father died of cancer and within a week of his death, his eldest daughter also died of cancer. This curse has now been broken in that family, and, in the past ten years, there has been no further evidence of this curse within the family.

24

Such experiences serve to illustrate the necessity for a ✓
deliverance ministry as a part of every pastor's care for his
people. For the first twenty years of my own pastoral
ministry, I was frustrated as a counselor. All I knew to tell
people was to read the Bible more, attend church regularly
and pray. Even when I gave them direct counsel from the
Word of God, it seldom changed their lives. That is why
I contend *that counseling alone is not enough to do the job.*
Counseling is effective only when coupled with discipline ✓ ✓
and deliverance. This is how my own family was able to
come out of its bondages and into spiritual unity, and it is
the only way I have been able to help others.

It is my prayer that every pastor will incorporate the
ministry of deliverance into his church. Church members
should not have to go outside their local fellowship to receive
salvation, the baptism in the Holy Spirit, healing, deliverance
or counseling.

One day Jesus was ministering. He cast out demons,
taught in the synagogue, preached the Gospel of the
Kingdom and healed every sickness and every disease among
the people. But He knew that these same people would have
continuing need.

> "And seeing the multitudes, He felt compassion for them,
> because they were distressed and downcast like sheep
> without a shepherd" (Matthew 9:36).

This is when Jesus urged his disciples to pray that the
Lord of the harvest would send forth laborers into His
harvest. Soon Jesus would go to the cross and return to the
Father's right hand. Laborers were needed. The very next
verse tells what He did to set the pattern for more workers.

> "And having summoned His twelve disciples, He gave
> them authority over unclean spirits, to cast them out, and
> to heal every kind of disease and every kind of sickness"
> (Matthew 10:1).

Jesus knew that preaching and teaching did not meet the
total needs of the people. They needed healing and deliver-

25

ance, too. He empowered the twelve and sent them out. They came back in a few days reporting their victory.

Families everywhere are crying out for help, the very kind of help Jesus gave people and commissioned His disciples to give them. We have been offered the same enduement of power that He gave the twelve.

Amen

> "For the promise is for you and your children, and for all who are far off, as many as the Lord our God shall call to Himself" (Acts 2:39).

Praise God, the resources for spiritual ministry did not die with the apostles! Pastors and people: The Lord is calling you to the labor of *the complete Gospel.* The fields are whiter than they have ever been. We must ALL work, for the night cometh when no man can work.

CHAPTER III

The Family in Prophecy

The condition of the earth's families in the last days is one of the chief signs given in the Bible to show us when the end is near. Right along with wars and rumors of wars, earthquakes, famine, pestilence and events in the Middle East, there is a prophesied breakdown in family relationships which causes family members to turn against one another. There is mounting evidence that the world is already witnessing the prelude to what God has foretold through His prophets.

Malachi's Prophecy

"Behold, I am going to send you Elijah the prophet before the coming of the great and terrible day of the Lord. And he will restore the hearts of the fathers to their children, and the hearts of the children to their fathers, lest I come and smite the land with a curse" (Malachi 4:5-6).

Here is a promise of an end-time restoration of the family. The family will be in desperate need of restoration. This means that the family will have experienced serious conflict and division requiring dramatic restoration. In fact, the condition of the earth's families will be so serious that an Elijah ministry will be required in order to avert a smiting judgment of God.

This Elijah ministry will come "before the coming of the great and terrible day of the Lord" (Malachi 4:5). The restoration of the family will precede the day when God's wrath is poured out upon the unrighteous. In the order of end-time events, tribulation precedes wrath. The Greek word for tribulation, *"thlipsis,"* means pressure. Pressures of every sort will increase. The scriptural analogy of the build-up of pressures is that of a pregnant woman entering into the final stages of childbirth. The labor pains grow in frequency and intensity. It will be a time of travail for the whole world. The family will experience this travail. Pressures will build up and families will be torn apart. Such widespread unrighteousness will prevail so that in order for anyone to escape the wrath of God, a mighty revival must take place. This revival will bring repentance to the families. The hearts of the fathers will be turned in love to their children, and the hearts of the children turned in obedience to their fathers. Only repentance turns the heart around. Such a revival will require a very strong ministry to bring it about, even the ministry of Elijah!

What are the earmarks of an Elijah ministry? First, we recall that Elijah's ministry was very bold. Elijah called everyone to a definite commitment: "If the Lord is God, follow Him" (I Kings 18:21). Sin was confronted, especially among those in leadership. Elijah came with the word of the Lord; he moved quickly and decisively. King Ahab's and Queen Jezebel's sins were exposed and condemned.

Futhermore, Elijah's ministry was *one of boldness in God.* When he prayed, things happened. Through prayer the rainfall in Israel ceased for three and a half years, and through prayer fire from heaven fell upon a water-soaked sacrifice. In the New Testament Elijah is used as an illustration of effective prayer; the kind of prayer necessary to bring forth healing.

Is God raising up such a ministry today? Cannot we agree that such a ministry is already needed? It will come as a ministry of confrontation. Those in authority, the false religionists, and all of the people will be confronted. This is what Elijah did. Confrontation forced each one to make a decision to either accept or reject the Lord. Then, along with the confrontation, was the display of God's power demonstrated through the effectual, fervent prayers of a righteous man. Just as the words of Jesus were evidenced by accompanying miracles, even so it was with Elijah's ministry, and so it will be with the upcoming Elijah ministry. God is going to require a definite decision on the part of parents and children. Will you obey God?

Secondly, Elijah's ministry was *a call to repentance.* God's people had fallen into the sin of idolatry. Their hearts were removed from allegiance to God. Their sins had separated them from God. Repentance is a doctrine that has not gone out of style. Repentance is as much needed today as at any time in human history. It is especially needed in our families. Parents need to repent of their sins against their children; not only their abuses, but also their neglects in failing to bring their children up in the nurture and admonition of the Lord. Children need to repent of their sins against their parents. Any child who has ever acted in disrespect and disobedience toward a parent has sinned against God. John the Baptist, whom Jesus said was a fulfillment of the Elijah prophesised by Malachi, confronted the false religious system of his day. In every generation there are false religious systems that arise to turn away the hearts of the people of God. John the Baptist, whom Jesus said was a fulfillment of the Elijah prophesied by Malachi, confronted the false religious system of the Scribes and Pharisees. He boldly challenged them saying, "You brood of vipers, who warned you to flee from the wrath to come? Therefore bring forth fruit in keeping with repentance" (Matthew 3:7-8). John's ministry demanded repentance as the condition for escape from the wrath of God. His ministry was that of a harbinger to prepare God's people for the coming of their Lord. (See Luke 1:17.) The coming Elijah ministry will serve the same purpose. God's people must be prepared to receive their King.

Secular humanism has become one of the strongest false religions of our day. It purports that man is god; he is the

MATT 3:7-8 29
LK 1:17

healer of his own ills. Secular humanism dismisses the need for God. The forces of secular humanism are at work in our public school system, in our universities and in our government (especially through lobbyists). Our children and youth are prime targets of secular humanism. Our families must be strong in the Lord if secular humanism's deadly influence upon our children is to be overcome. The church and the family are headed for direct confrontation with principalities, world rulers of darkness and spiritual wickedness in high places. An Elijah ministry is needed to lead us in the overthrow of all such dark spiritual forces that are seeking to frustrate and eliminate all godly influence from the lives of our youth. Shall God's people stand idly by as God is banned from the classroom? Shall our children be forbidden to pray? Shall our teachers be forbidden to teach God's creation and instead be required to teach an atheistic evolution concocted and supported by those who "do not like to retain God in their knowledge," and who are destined to be given over to a "reprobate mind"? (Romans 1:28).

The emerging Elijah ministry is leading the way in spiritual warfare. It is not a fleshly confrontation but a spiritual one. It is like Moses and Aaron confronting Pharoah's magicians in the demonstration and power of God's Spirit. The family's role in spiritual warfare must not be overlooked. Jesus declared that His church would be a militant church against whose mighty power the very gates of hell would be unable to stand. (See Matthew 16:18.) It is not only the church, but also the family who must defeat the enemy in his gates. The family and the church are intricately related. The "gates of Hell" represent the strategies of the devil, his plans and his wiles. The place and time to offset the devil's plans against us are in his "gates." In ancient times the gates of a city were the place of city government. It was here that the counsels of war were devised. Who is to take the offensive against the strategies of the devil and defeat him in his gates? The church? Yes, but also the family.

30

"Unless the Lord builds the house,
They labor in vain who would build it. . .
Behold, children are a gift of the Lord;
The fruit of the womb is a reward.
Like arrows in the hand of a warrior,
So are the children of one's youth.
How blessed is the man whose quiver is full of them;
They shall not be ashamed,
When they speak with [literally, subdue; destroy]*
Their enemies in the gate" (Psalms 127:3-5).

Again, consider the promise of God to Abraham that his family would possess the gate of the enemy.

"Indeed I will greatly bless you, and I will greatly multiply your seed as the stars of the heavens, and as the sand which is on the seashore; and your seed shall possess the gate of their enemies" (Genesis 22:17).

Again let us note the prophetic prayer spoken over Rebekah by her family when they sent her away to become the wife of Isaac.

"And they blessed Rebekah and said to her, 'May you, our sister, become thousands of ten thousands, And may your descendants possess the gate of those who hate them' " (Genesis 24:60).

There is no need for today's family to be torn apart and destroyed by the workings of Satan. The family must seriously enter into spiritual warfare and take the offensive against the gates of hell. The family must be in unity with the full cooperation of each of its members. This will require extreme diligence in the ways of God.

Paul's Prophecy

"But realize this, that in the last days difficult times will come. For men will be lovers of self, lovers of money, boastful, arrogant, revilers, DISOBEDIENT TO PARENTS,** ungrateful, unholy, unloving, irreconcilable,

**Emphasis mine.

31

malicious gossips, without self-control, brutal, haters of good, treacherous, reckless, conceited, lovers of pleasure rather than lovers of God; holding to a form of godliness, although they have denied its power; and avoid such men as these" (II Timothy 3:1-5).

These described conditions will worsen as the day of the Lord approaches. The only way they can worsen is through the breakdown of the family. The parents are responsible before God for instilling spiritual and moral principles in the hearts and lives of their children. When the world is characterized by the terrible conditions described in this passage, it can only mean that the family has miserably failed in its basic duty to bring up children in the Lord.

One key phrase points to the root of the problem: "disobedient to parents." Children will become rebellious and unteachable. Children are the product of the home. We have been assured by God's Word that when we bring up a child in the way he should go, when he is old he will not depart from it. When children go astray, the responsibility rests squarely on the shoulders of the parents.

Jesus' Prophecy

"And at that time many will fall away and will deliver up one another and hate one another" (Matthew 24:10).

"And a brother will deliver brother to death, and a father his child; and children will rise up against parents and have them put to death" (Mark 13:12).

"But you will be delivered up even by parents and brothers and relatives and friends, and they will put some of you to death" (Luke 21:16).

In these three parallel accounts Jesus has given us a glimpse of the total chaos that shall overtake the family prior to His return. Each of the Gospel accounts emphasizes betrayal of family members against one another. This betrayal will result in the deaths of parents and children. What shall have become of family love and loyalty? It is difficult to imagine such things, much less to consider that they could soon be realized in our own homes.

The importance of getting one's family into Kingdom living becomes ever increasingly urgent as we are faced with these scripture evidences of coming pressures upon the world that will directly affect every family. To have our families in Divine order becomes a matter of survival.

Isaiah's Prophecy

"And the people will be oppressed, Each one by another, and each one by his neighbor; The young will storm against the elder, And the inferior against the honorable. . . O My people! Their oppressors are children, And women rule over them. O My people! Those who guide you lead you astray, And confuse the direction of your paths" (Isaiah 3:5-12).

Isaiah pictures the breakdown of family government and the results. When discipline and respect are no longer taught in the home, there will be an atmosphere of total oppression. Everyone will be doing his own thing and looking out for himself at the expense and disregard of everyone else.

Have you known families whose members tear one another apart rather than build up one another? Some families have become like a chicken yard when cannibalism sets in. Chickens sometimes begin to peck one another. When blood appears, every chicken in the yard becomes a killer. They literally peck one another to death. This kind of condition already exists in some Christian homes. When one member of the family is "down," it seems to be time for all the others to jump on him. But how different and beautiful when a family learns to support one another and come to the assistance of the member that is suffering or faltering. For example, if mother is overloaded in responsibilities and may even be tired or weak, this is an opportunity for all the family members to come to her support. When love is the atmosphere in the home, then everyone

33

will work in cooperation and support one another. The unity of love should be the same in the natural family as is required in the spiritual family, the church!

> ". . . from whom the whole body, being fitted and held together by that which every joint supplies, according to the proper working of each individual part, causes the growth of the body for the building up of itself in love" (Ephesians 4:16).

Respect for one another is one of the most important things for a family to cultivate. Husbands and wives must maintain respect for one another. This loss of respect is one of the first signs of trouble in the home. Children will be taught respect for others principally through the example of their parents.

Disrespect in the home cannot be confined to the home. Soon it will become manifest outside the home. The whole nation or society will be affected. The government of a people will then be unable to rule where people have lost respect for the elderly, the wise, and those in authority. This is why God wrote into the Ten Commandments, with His own finger, the commandment with promise:

> "Honor your father and mother, that your days may be prolonged in the land which the Lord your God gives you" (Exodus 20:12).

Isaiah foretells a national condition of such rebellion and anarchy that no man wants to assume leadership; in fact, men refuse to be coerced into leadership. The men have all become renegades and "women rule over them." (See Isaiah 3:6-7,12.) There is nothing any plainer in the Bible than that God has ordained men to assume headship in the home, the church and the nation. Today, more and more women are forced to bear responsibilities of headship that God never intended them to carry and for which He did not equip them. This is why the rule of women is spoken of as a judgment upon the nation.

All of these prophecies concerning the family in the last

days should be received as a warning from God. To be forewarned should result in preparedness or else the warning has fallen on deaf ears. The trumpet call of the Lord to His people in this hour is preparedness. The writer of Hebrews says that the time to get prepared is before the shaking starts.

> "See to it that you do not refuse Him who is speaking. For if those did not escape when they refused him who warned them on earth, much less shall we escape who turn away from Him who warns from heaven. And His voice shook the earth then, but now He has promised, saying 'Yet once more I will shake not only the earth, but also the heaven.' And this expression, 'Yet once more,' denotes the removing of those things which can be shaken, as of created things, in order that those things which cannot be shaken may remain. Therefore, since we receive a kingdom which cannot be shaken, let us show gratitude, by which we may offer to God an acceptable service with reverence and awe; for our God is a consuming fire" (Hebrews 13:25-29).

CHAPTER IV

Family Goals

After thirty-four years of pastoring and marriage counseling, I am convinced that an overwhelming majority of married people just stumble into marriage. They become married with little or no forethought. Too few marriages are truly formed in the Lord. Even the marriages of Christian people, brought up in the church, are seldom the result of prayer and seeking the will of God. No wonder there are so many marriage failures.

The preparation for successful marriage begins in childhood and continues through adolescence. The best insurance for a good marriage is for a child to be brought up in a stable home, where parents love one another and love their children, where the principles of God's Word are practiced; and the children have a daily example of what a real marriage should be.

Both good and bad home-lives have a way of perpetuating themselves. Those who come from good homes are prone to build good homes for themselves. This is as it should be expected, for the Bible says, ''. . . Train up a child in the way he should go, Even when he is old he will not depart from it'' (Proverbs 22:6). On the other hand, there are those who have no Christian example placed before them; they are surrounded by instability. How can they be expected to build something that they have never known?

My own home upbringing serves as a good example of what I am saying. My parents brought me up in the nuture and admonition of the Lord. My father was a Baptist deacon

36

and respected leader in the church all of his life. We always had a family altar in our home. My two brothers and I knew we were not to leave the breakfast table each morning until father had led the family in Bible reading and prayer. We regularly attended all church meetings. However, I learned more Bible doctrine and Christian principles of life at home than I did through Sunday school and church. Later, when I went off to work and then into the army, I knew that my parents were praying for me each day. I met with many temptations and opportunities to walk in sinful ways, but the truth that had been instilled in my heart kept me in the ways of God.

My father came from a good family. My grandfather Hammond was a pillar in the church and an upstanding man in the community. So, my father had a good example to follow, and I had a good example to follow. I have two brothers. Neither my brothers nor I have ever smoked, drank or gone the way of the world. All are active in the Body of Christ. We have one daughter, and she has always been a special blessing to us as parents. She loves the Lord and follows in His ways. The godly heritage is being passed down.

As a general rule of thumb, the more stable the home the more stable the children. What then can be done for those who come from homes where parents were not Christians and personalities were warped? This is where the grace of God comes in. On the one hand, the devil is doing all he can to destroy families; but, on the other hand, God is at work restoring families. In Christ Jesus no one needs to remain a prisoner of his past. In Him old things pass away, and all things become new. In Him we forget those things which are behind and press toward the mark of the high calling of God in Christ Jesus. In Him there is deliverance. He brings us into His Kingdon of righteousness, peace and joy.

PREMARRIAGE GOALS

I was visiting in a church where someone had a vision of the church's ministry. He saw a church built at the bottom of a cliff. People kept falling over the cliff and being injured. The church was ministering to all those who were broken and bruised. Then a church was seen built at the top of the cliff, and its ministry was to keep people from falling over the cliff and being injured. Surely, the church has the responsibility to minister at both ends of the spectrum. There is one thing better than effective ministry that restores broken homes: a ministry that prevents homes from becoming broken. Both ministries are essential. While we minister to those who have fallen over the cliff, let us not forget those who have not. Let us train them in disciplined living and walking in the Spirit, so that they will never fall.

By the time our children come to marriageable age, their hearts should be crystalized in spiritual principles governing marriage. They should have definite goals for marriage. The first goal should be, "I will marry in the Lord." This means that a believer will not marry an unbeliever. This Scripture is plain: "Do not be bound together with unbelievers" (II Corinthians 6:14). This principle has a wider application than marriage, but it definitely applies to marriage. With this goal fixed in the heart, no believer would permit himself to entertain the thought of marrying someone who is other than a born-again believer. No marriage can function in true spiritual unity unless both husband and wife love the Lord with all their hearts, souls, minds, and all of their strength.

False compassion has drawn many an individual into an unequally yoked marriage. For example, a young woman, dedicated to Christ meets a man who is lost. He drinks and gambles and commits fornication. She is deceived into thinking that she is his salvation, and, that through her influence, he will become a different person if she marries him. So, she marries this man in contradiction to the Word of God.

One who is wise respects the counsel of God by obedience to His Word. "The fear of the Lord is the beginning of wisdom" (Psalms 111:10). There are too many hellish marriages where this counsel of God was not followed.

I have also seen the blessing that comes to those who adhere to God's counsel not to marry outside the Lord. I have seen those who turned down opportunities to marry an unbeliever in order to wait for God's timing and God's provision of a spouse. These refused to lower the standard, and God gave them good partners. Some readers of this book may be exceptions or know of others who are exceptions to what I have just said. If so, you owe a special prayer of thanksgiving unto the Lord for a spouse who now accepts and follows the Lord in spite of your disobedience in becoming unequally yoked.

A fifteen year old girl was visiting in our home, and she had asked permission to use my typewriter. Later, she handed me a typed page that listed seventeen things she expected in the husband God would give her. First, he must be born again, filled with the Spirit, and he must walk in the ways of God. Every young man and young woman should have such standards in their hearts and believe God to bring that person into his or her life. Those who put their trust in God will never be disappointed.

The following goals for marriage were taken from lists submitted by young people during a family seminar at Philadelphia Fellowship, Metairie, Louisiana:

THE ONE I MARRY MUST BE:

1. Born again –

2. Baptized in the Holy Spirit –

3. Manifesting the power of the Holy Spirit –

4. Filled with the fruit of the Holy Spirit –

5. Loving God supremely –

6. Setting a good Christian example in life

7. Spiritually disciplined in Bible study, prayer and fasting

8. An active member of the Body of Christ

9. Sexually pure and modest

10. Trustworthy and faithful

11. Honest and sincere

12. Walking in faith

13. A good communicator

14. Teachable

15. Industrious

16. Given to hospitality

17. Well-groomed

18. Disciplined in good hygiene

19. Disciplined in eating habits

20. Disciplined in finances

21. Patient with others

22. A person with vision and purpose in life

Having one's goal for marriage "in the Lord" will cause one to see his potential spouse with the eyes of God. With God, inward beauty is a priority above outward beauty. The "Proverbs Woman" described in Proverbs 31 is the ideal kind of wife for every God-fearing young man. She is the wife that God approves. It is said of her:

"Charm and grace are deceptive, and beauty is vain [because it is not lasting], but a woman who reverently and worshipfully fears the Lord, she shall be praised!" (Proverbs 31:30, Amplified Bible).

According to I Peter 3:4-5, a woman is of beauty and great

price in the sight of God if she has adorned her inward self with a meek and quiet spirit and genuinely puts her trust in God.

A second major goal for premarriage is: "I will keep myself pure." Everyone can agree that it is easier today than formerly for individuals to have premarital sex due to such things as the automobile and the pill, but God still calls it fornication. One still cannot sow unto the flesh without reaping corruption. The world may change its morals, but God does not change His Word. Sin of any sort will open the door for demons to enter and eventually bring the judgment of God. Fornication is a sin against one's own body, and it damages that person's relationship with God through the loss of fellowship. As Paul says,

> "Flee immorality. Every other sin that a man commits is outside the body, but the immoral man sins against his own body. Or do you not know that your body is a temple of the Holy Spirit who is in you, whom you have from God, and that you are not your own? For you have been bought with a price: therefore glorify God in your body" (I Corinthians 6:18-20).

Premarital sex will have its repercussions throughout marriage, whether a husband and wife have had sex with one another before marriage or with other persons. It should be understood that fornication is an expression of lust, not love. Individuals who have not had satisfying love in childhood are prone to seek love satisfaction in illegitimate ways. The devil's counterfeit for love is lust. Love satisfies but lust does not.

A satisfying relationship between a man and a woman must be based on the right kind of love. The Greek language uses several different words to express the different meanings of love. "Agape" is the first word for love. It is the word used to describe God's love for us. God's love is characterized by the action it prompts. Agape love is a sacrificial love; it is totally unselfish. Lust is rooted in selfishness. It is motivated by the desire to gratify one's own carnal appetite.

It is the opposite of agape love. Agape love honors and values purity. Agape love "does not act unbecomingly; it does not seek its own" (I Corinthians 13:5). A man who has this kind of love toward a woman will not endanger her nor disgrace her.

A second Greek word for love is "phileo." In distinction from agape, phileo love represents affectionate love which is warm, tender and thoughtful. It is the kind of love that a mother is to have toward her children. (See Titus 2:4.) This is an acceptable kind of premarital love.

The third Greek word for love is "eros." This word is not found in the New Testament but was used by the Greeks to describe love that is absorbed in sexual desire. From eros we get our English word "erotic," meaning that which arouses sexual desire. It is the love that is stimulated by petting. Eros love, then, is the road to fornication.

Here are some of the repercussions that follow in the wake of premarital sex:

1. Used feeling. A woman feels used rather than loved. After she has yielded her body for intended love; thereafter, she will question the motive of the man and conclude that he did not really love her but only wanted her body.

2. Rejection. Rejection is experienced when love is questioned. Suppose the woman becomes pregnant out of wedlock and then the two decide to get married. Did he marry her because he loved her or because he just felt obligated? She can never really be sure. These thoughts create disrespect toward the husband and sometimes cause frigidity in the wife.

3. Distrust. If individuals are unable to keep themselves pure before marriage, how can they trust one another to keep themselves pure after marriage? Is he/she the kind of person I can really trust?

4. Guilt. Unless the conscience is completely seared, a person cannot help having a guilty conscience over having

committed fornication. Some individuals' guilt and condemnation over sexual sin have caused them to fall into deep depression with suicidal tendencies and have even resulted in insanity.

5. Fear. There can be the fear of pregnancy out of wedlock and all the assorted problems that could arise from it. There may be the fear of exposure: what will parents and others close to me think of me? If a child is actually conceived, what will be the effect on him if he ever discovers that he was conceived before marriage?

These are not imaginary repercussions from premarital sex, but they represent case history after case history of those to whom we have ministered and who are suffering from the results of fornication in its impact upon their minds, emotions, bodies and spirits.

One sin often leads to another as it did with King David when he commited murder in an attempt to conceal his sexual sin. Likewise, abortion is the sin of murder, and it compounds the sin of fornication.*

Not only is the woman who has had an abortion guilty of murder, but also the one who caused it, performs it or agrees with it. Jesus taught that murder begins with heart attitude. We need forgiveness and deliverance from sins we have agreed with in our hearts. Anyone who agrees with abortion, has agreed with murder and needs God's forgiveness.**

Unconfessed and unrepented sins can block deliverance. Abortion is a commonly unconfessed sin, because so many have not considered it to be a sin. In the Old Testament there was a blood sacrifice offered for the sins of ignorance. This sacrifice was offered in case a person had committed a sin

---

*Fornication is a broad designation for all illicit sexual intercourse including not only premarital sex but also adultery, bestiality, homosexuality and incest.

**For a fuller discussion of abortion we recommend, *Ministering to Abortion's Aftermath* by Bill and Sue Banks, obtainable through Impact Books, 137 West Jefferson, Kirkwood Missouri 63122.

without realizing it. It is to be noted that the sacrificial blood of Jesus is required for the atonement of our sins, whether or not we recognize them as sins.

Through the prophet Isaiah, God warned of the day when men would call good evil and evil good. (See Isaiah 5:20.) Abortion is a case in point. For the first twenty years of my ministry, I did not have a clear-cut conviction about abortion. One thing that involvement in deliverance ministry does for a person is to remove the gray areas of sin so that everything becomes black or white.

One day my wife and I were ministering to a woman whom we had just met. Immediately, the Lord revealed to us that she had had an abortion. She admitted that she had. After we shared with her that God considered it as the sin of murder, she asked and received God's forgiveness. Then we commanded the companion demons of abortion and murder to come out of her. The demons manifested themselves by creating a very strong pressure and swelling around her throat. For several moments her breath was cut off, and the pressure became so intense that small blood vessels around her throat and lower face began to rupture.* Then, something flew out of her mouth and into a wastebasket which had been placed in front of her. There in the basket was a spot of bright red blood the size of a silver dollar. Next to it was a perfectly formed, fleshly embryo which was the exact size and shape of one that would be about three months in formation. The demons of murder and abortion had materialized!

This experience is inserted at this point to emphasize the importance of keeping oneself pure before marriage. It is the way to keeping oneself free of demonization and from the defilements of sin.

---

*In several instances where Jesus cast out demons they were said to "tear" the person since they resisted being cast out. (See Mark 1:26; 9:20-26; Luke 4:35.)

GOALS FOR HUSBANDS AND WIVES

Goals are important, and they are scriptural. The Apostle Paul was a great one for establishing goals for himself. Here is one of his goals that is important for every married couple:

Forgetting the Past

". . . but one thing I do: forgetting what lies behind and reaching forward to what lies ahead, I press on toward the goal for the prize of the upward call of God in Christ Jesus" (Philippians 3:13-14).

One thing that can keep us from pressing on is our failure to forget those things which are behind. Husbands and wives have accumulated their shares of "mental garbage." Some of it was prior to marriage, and some of it subsequent to marriage. If either one or both of them continue to dwell upon the past, it will prevent them from being bonded together in Christ.

For the sake of illustration, let us say that a husband at one time was unfaithful to his wife. If he has repented of his sin and received God's forgiveness, the wife is required by God to forgive him also. (See Luke 17:3-4.) If the wife continues to "throw it up to him," she is keeping the matter alive and preventing a healing of their relationship.

"If you forgive the sins of any, their sins have been forgiven them; if you retain the sins of any, they have been retained" (John 20:23).

In other words, if we lay hold of some sin another person has committed, that sin is retained and kept alive. The way God removes sin from our lives is by forgiving it; the way we remove sin that is among ourselves is by forgiving one another.

When my wife and I began to receive our deliverance from things in the past, we were required by God to deal with things in our past relationship which had not been settled through forgiveness. Although we did not talk to one another about hurts and differences which had occurred between us, these matters were buried inside us like embers that appear dead on the outside but inside are alive and ready to burst into flame with only a little fanning or fuel.

We had to recognize that we are not today what we once were. We have grown and matured in the Lord. We can no longer view one another and judge one another on the basis of previous immaturity. Yes, we have both made some mistakes; and we have hurt one another at times, but we are not bound by that. If we dwell on past hurts, we will be imprisioned by our memories and will miss the glories of walking with Christ today.

So, our goal is to forget all the past hurts and sins which have been washed away by the atoning blood of Jesus Christ, and to change all of our former ways of hurting one another and to walk in love.

> "Let all bitterness and wrath and anger and clamor and slander be put away from you, along with all malice. And be kind to one another, tender-hearted, forgiving each other, just as God in Christ also has forgiven you. Therefore be imitators of God, as beloved children; and walk in love, just as Christ also loved you, and gave Himself up for us . . ." (Ephesians 4:31-32; 5:2a).

Divine Order

God has established a certain order of government for the family. God has said that "the husband is the head of the wife" (Ephesians 5:23). The way that the wife recognizes and honors the husband's headship is through her submission to the husband. This form of family government is not optional; it is an absolute requirement for all who expect to enjoy Kingdom living. This form of family government and this form alone is approved by God. We do not have the privilege of changing God's order to one of our own devising. The husband's headship is an extension of Divine authority, a direct function of the Kingdom of God.

Since this matter of Divine order is treated fully in the following chapters on "The Husband's Headship" and "The Wife's Submission," I will reserve further comment until that time. It needs to be noted in reference to goals, that the husband and wife must be in right order or nothing else will work.

One Flesh

The relationship between Christ and His church is the pattern of relationship between husband and wife. Christ and His church are "one."

> "For this cause a man shall leave his father and mother, and shall cleave to his wife; and the two shall become one flesh" (Ephesians 5:31).

The phase "one flesh" denotes one in relationship. It is much more than that which is brought about through sexual union. It is the complete bonding of spirit, soul and body. When a couple stands before a minister to exchange their vows of covenant relationship, we may hear the minister say, "I now pronounce you husband and wife; what God, therefore, hath joined together, let no man put asunder." Thereafter, the process begins of working out what God has worked in. It is comparable to the spiritual inheritance we receive in Christ at the moment of salvation. We have it all in embryo form, but it is not ours experientially. Neither the wedding vows nor the honeymoon bring complete oneness between husband and wife; the oneness is realized through a disciplinary process.

"But the one who joins himself to the Lord is one spirit with Him" (I Corinthians 6:17). That is, his spiritual heartbeat is the same as the Lord's. The word "joined" is the same word that speaks of the husband being joined to his wife. The Greek work literally means "glued, bonded or cemented." A man joined unto the Lord will leave all other gods and be of one spirit with the Lord. Likewise, the man joined to his wife will leave all other relationships and be of one spirit with her.

Spiritual oneness is strengthened by functioning together spiritually. Joint Bible study, prayer, fasting, worship, praise and giving are ways of functioning as one spirit. The primary function of husband and wife is spiritual. Their lives together are to glorify God. If a couple has married in the Lord, it means they have married in order to fulfill God's will. They will recognize that God has a purpose for them as a couple. Only by functioning together in spiritual ways will they recognize and realize the spiritual goal. No matter what other accomplishments a couple may attain, there will never be a sense of wholeness and life fulfillment.

Physical oneness comes by doing physical things together. This includes but involves much more than the marriage bed. Joint physical projects might be jogging, walking or tennis for exercise or work projects such as gardening, redecorating the house or cleaning the attic. Marriage should solve one of man's biggest problems: being alone. God saw that it was not good for man to be alone, and that is when Eve was created as a companion. Marriage is a covenant of companionship.

Unless a couple does things together, they can easily drift apart. A husband may stay busy at his job; and his wife may stay busy keeping up the housework and the children, but they must find time to cultivate togetherness. The temptation to find companionship elsewhere is created by the neglect of companionship between husband and wife.

Oneness of soul is cultivated by communication. Failure to talk things over is at the bottom of many unhappy marriages; walls of division are built and stress created. Lack of meaningful and healthy communication is lacking in so many marriages that, as a marriage counselor, I have found myself asking, "Why don't husbands and wives communicate?" I believe the main reason is the simple fact that they never learned how.

48

If a person comes from a family that does not communicate, then that person has never learned how. If anything, the family I was brought up in over-communicated. The smallest details of everything that went on were hashed and rehashed. If we were to take an automobile ride, there would be prolonged discussion about the weather, the clothing to be worn and the route to take. When I married, I took the same pattern of communication into our marriage; rather, I attempted to do so. The problem was that my wife had come from the opposite type of home. If her family took a short automobile ride, everyone jumped in the car and off they went. Her parents had very little communication, so she had never learned how. Too much communication on my part wearied her and too little on her part frustrated me. It took a while, but eventually we were able to reach a happy medium.

Another hindrance to communication is fear. It might be the fear of rejection, of criticism, of not being understood, of hurt, of confrontation or of unpleasantness. The last things that my wife submitted to me were her inner thoughts and private opinions. There was a fear of how I would react. Would I laugh at her, scold her or ignore what she said? She could not communicate her inner self until she could trust me to handle it right. Who wants to talk if what is said touches off conflict?

Unhindered Prayer

We can understand why the devil hates unity between a husband and wife when we realize the spiritual power that is created when two pray together in agreement. The most natural combination of two people praying together is that of two who have become "one flesh."

> "Again I say to you, that if two of you agree on earth about anything that they may ask, it shall be done for them by My Father who is in heaven" (Matthew 18:19).

The verb *"agree"* is *"sumphoneo"* in Greek. It is a term used of musical instruments when they are in tune and sound together in accord. The agreement required then is more than mere mental assent; the two must be in complete heart agreement.

Two basic conditions must be met before a husband and wife can pray in one accord. First, the wife must be in submission to her husband. She must agree with him. Have you observed how one musical instrument tunes to another so that they will be able to play together without disharmony? In the church where I pastor, a number of instruments are used. Before each service, all the stringed instruments are tuned to the piano. Since the husband is the "head of the wife," the wife tunes to her husband which enables them to sound their prayers in unity. In turn, the piano is tuned to standard pitch which represents the husband's accord with the will of God. "Christ is the head of every man" (I Corinthians 11:3).

For many years my wife and I worked independently of one another in most spiritual things. She had her Bible study, and I had mine. She did her own praying, and I did mine. Now these spiritual activities are blended together. She discovered that the quickest way for us to reach agreement in prayer was for her to inquire of me, "How do you feel impressed of the Lord to pray about a certain matter?" Then she would reply, "I agree with that."

The second condition for united prayer is on the part of the husband.

> "You husbands likewise, live with your wives in an understanding way, as with a weaker vessel, since she is a woman; and grant her honor as a fellow heir of the grace of life, so that your prayers may not be hindered" (I Peter 3:7).

The "understanding way" in which the husband relates to the wife is for the purpose of creating a oneness of relationship. He knows her in love as one deserving of respect

50

and special protection. He understands her as one who is of equal importance with himself in the eyes of God for she is "a fellow heir of the grace of life." The wife will find it easy to agree with a husband who relates to her with the same kind of loving understanding that Christ has for the church.

Thus, the prayer goal for husband and wife is to remain in such one-accordness that they will be able to agree about everything in prayer at any time of day or night. The slightest break in relationship between the two will break the power of prayer. Therefore, anything that clouds the relationship must be remedied speedily. If the prayer lines are down, the power of united prayer is lost until they are restored.

Sexual Purity and Compatibility

The devil gets into a marriage through the bedroom more frequently than any other opening. If things do not go right in the marriage bed, all other facets of relationships are tainted.

There are many reasons why married persons have problems relating sexually. Here are some of them:

1. Teaching from childhood that all sex is dirty

2. Guilt and condemnation due to premarital sex

3. Punishment of the spouse by withholding sexual rights

4. Control of the spouse by "I will give you sex if you give me . . ."

5. Fear of pregnancy

6. Frigidity due to molestation or incest in childhood

7. Wife's inability to climax

8. Husband's impotency (which can be physical or emotional)

9. Unreasonable sexual demands by one's spouse

10. "Burn out" due to excessive fornication prior to marriage

11. Fear of pain (the wife may have yeast infection or other conditions that may make intercourse painful)

12. Lack of bedroom privacy (children sleeping in the room or nearby)

13. Lack of hygiene (unbrushed teeth, unbathed body, unwashed hair)

14. Perverted sex (oral or anal) insisted upon by one's spouse

Demons of sexual frustration and sexual rejection are not uncommon when sexual needs are not satisfied. This is why the Scripture admonishes:

> "The husband should give to his wife her conjugal rights. . . For the wife does not have [exclusive] authority and control over her own body, but the husband [has his rights]; likewise also the husband does not have [exclusive] authority and control over his body, but the wife [has her rights]. Do not refuse and deprive and defraud each other (of your due marital rights), except perhaps by mutual consent for a time, that you may devote yourselves unhindered to prayer. But afterwards resume marital relations, lest Satan tempt you [to sin] through your lack of restraint of sexual desire" (I Corinthians 7:3a,4-5 Amplified Bible).

Sexual purity is also an important goal. Sexual impurity and perverseness must be avoided in the marriage bed. Hebrews 13:4 has been wrongly interpreted by some as meaning "anything goes" between husband and wife. Let us examine that verse.

"Let marriage be held in honor — esteemed worthy, precious, [that is], of great price and especially dear — in all things. And thus let the marriage bed be (kept undishonored), undefiled; for God will judge and punish the unchaste (all guity of sexual vice) and adulterous" (Hebrews 13:4, Amplified Bible).

Notice that the verb action has been corrected from the King James translation. Instead of reading, "the marriage bed is undefiled," it is correctly rendered in the Amplified, "let the marriage bed be undefiled." The bed is not automatically undefiled but can become defiled by wrong practices. The word translated "whoremongers" in the King James version is translated "unchaste" in the Amplified. The Greek word is "pornos" and is the common word for fornicator. Fornication is a broad term embracing the sexual sins of premarital sex, adultery, bestiality, homosexuality and sodomy. Fornication can take place between a husband and wife through perverseness. Oral sex and anal sex are forms of sodomy, for sodomy is either unnatural carnal copulation between persons of the same sex or between persons of the opposite sex.

Oral sex is practiced by homosexuals and lesbians. This unclean practice opens a person to unclean spirits of the same nature. We ministered to a woman who was well known in Christian circles for her godly works and influence. She confided in us that she had become involved in a lesbian affair. Upon questioning her, we discovered that her husband required oral sex between them. She had been opened to the spirit of lesbianism through the practice of oral sex with her husband. We have found this pattern repeated in other instances.

When demons are cast out, they sometimes manifest themselves by demonstrating the behavior they cause. For example, the spirit of pride may be manifested by the lifting of a person's head or puffing out of his chest. The demon of oral sex sometimes manifests itself in the mouth and tongue of the person receiving deliverance with sucking and licking actions. Once these manifestations are witnessed in deliverance, all doubt is removed as to the perverseness of oral sex between husband and wife. Even nature itself tells us oral sex is wrong. Herpes, a difficult to control form of venereal disease, is contracted and spread through oral sex.

Purity of marital sexual relations can also become polluted through engaging in sexual relationship at the time of the wife's menstrual flow.

> "If there is a man who lies with a menstrous woman and uncovers her nakedness, he has laid bare her flow, and she has exposed the flow of her blood; thus both of them shall be cut off from among their people" (Leviticus 20:18).

The husband, therefore, must not be demanding upon his wife at the time of her monthly cycle but practice continence. Since violation of God's Word is sin and sin brings a curse, a couple's sexual life may be bound under a curse if they have so sinned. Although one may have done such things in ignorance, now he has come into the light and God requires repentance.

Financial Cooperation

Conflict over financial matters is another door-opener to the enemy. Both husband and wife must be disciplined in the handling of money. If either has entered into marriage without such discipline, then discipline should be a major personal goal. Some persons never learned to handle money as they grew up. If one does not control money, it will soon control him.

A family budget is helpful in promoting disciplined spending. Credit cards are a "no-no" for undisciplined spenders. They make it too easy to over-charge. The resulting indebtedness can strain a marriage in a hurry.

Some people need to be delivered from spirits of material lust before they can successfully discipline themselves. Lust is never satisfied. A lust demon is never satiated by gaining more material things.

Here in the United States, and wherever there is a high standard of living, an overevaluation can easily be placed on money and what money can buy. Money must be gained and used, not as an end in itself, but as an avenue of laying up treasure in heaven. Meditate upon these Sriptures:

"Do not lay up for yourselves treasures upon earth, where moth and rust destroy, and where thieves break in and steal. . . for where your treasure is, there will your heart be also" (Matthew 6:19-21).

"For those who are according to the flesh set their minds on the things of the flesh, but those who are according to the Spirit, the things of the Spirit. For the mind set on the flesh is death, but the mind set on the Spirit is life and peace" (Romans 8:5-6).

"What is the source of quarrels and conflicts among you? Is not the source your pleasures that wage war in your members? You lust and do not have; so you commit murder. And you are envious and cannot obtain; so you fight and quarrel. You do not have because you do not ask. You ask and do not receive, because you ask with wrong motives, so that you may spend it on your pleasures" (James 4:1-3).

Indeed, many of the wars and fightings within the family are due to unconquered lust for things. The way to acquire what we need is not through fighting but through prayer and faith.

Material prosperity comes from God. It is a benefit of Kingdom living. Poverty is a curse. Anyone not enjoying the flow of "milk and honey" has not yet reached Caanan.

Husband and wife must learn to share. Selfishness creates stress and conflict.

". . . being of the same mind, maintaining the same love, united in spirit, intent on one purpose. Do nothing from selfishness or empty conceit, but with humility of mind let each of you regard one another as more important than himself; do not merely look out for your own personal interests, but also for the interests of others" (Philippians 2:2-4).

We have already mentioned the importance of communication. Working out finances requires a great deal of communicating. Communication is not productive when it generates more heat than light.

It is "a more excellent way" when the wife does not have to work outside the home to provide money for family needs, especially when children need her care. If material things are gained at the expense of a child's need for his parent, the price is too high.

Having experienced the "before and after" of my wife working in the world to help support the family, I would personally make it a priority in prayer for God to give financial adequacy without the wife's added income.

One further word about family finances: Husbands will be wise not to put unnecessary and unfair burdens on their wives by turning the paycheck over to them, thus expecting them to make all of the financial decisions. Husbands sometimes do this to escape personal responsibility and then blame the wife if the money runs short.

Edification

Since marriage brings two people into such close relationship (the two become one), everything one does affects the other. Even each spoken word carries power to either build up or tear down.

The word "edify" in various forms occurs several times in the New Testament. It is a translation of "oikodome" from "oikos" (home) and "demo" (build), which literally means "building a home." How significant! Edification is the process of building a home. It represents all the ways in which those in a home build up the home by building up one another. The physical building process parallels the spiritual. This causes us to ask: What is required to build a solid home?

Planning: The blue print is the Word of God, drawn up by the Master Architect and Builder. God's Word contains all of the specifications needed to build a solid marriage. God Himself will remain the Consultant throughout the building process. Adopting goals for marriage is the acceptance of God's plan for building the home.

Good Materials: These represent good works and deeds. They are the same as the fruits of the Spirit: love, joy, peace, longsuffering, gentleness, goodness, faith, meekness and temperance (Galatians 5:22-23). Love is the mortar which holds everything together.

Skills: Skill is acquired by experience. When a young couple begin to build their home, they are entering upon something that they have never done before. They must depend upon the One who does have the skill to teach them step by step. "Unless the Lord builds the house, they labor in vain who build it" (Psalm 127:1).

Labor: Buildings do not just happen. Each one required much hard work. Anyone who builds a house must be committed to staying with it until it is complete. The last part of building a house is called "the finishing work," which involves all the trim. The finishing work adds beauty and grace. This represents the detailed work that goes into making a beautiful marriage.

> "So then let us pursue the things which make for peace and the building up of one another" (Romans 14:19).

Commitment

Marriage is a covenant relationship. The covenant represents an agreement, a pledge or commitment which obligates a husband and a wife to one another. The vows are the terms of the covenant; they reflect the hearts of love that each has for the other. They involve the setting aside of previous ties in order to form a new and lasting tie. A man will leave his father and mother and will cleave unto his wife, and the wife will leave the covering of her parents and be joined unto her own husband. They will make all other human relationships secondary to their own.

A genuine commitment to one another creates a security that wards off many a demon. A beautiful example of this occurred in the lives of a young couple who were about to experience the birth of their first child. The young woman was in the final stages of labor and her husband told her, "I want you to know that you are first in my life. I don't expect anything to happen to the baby, but I want you to know that you are first." As it turned out there was a serious complication, and the moment the baby was born he was rushed to intensive care. The young husband remained with his wife in the birthing room to comfort and strengthen her with his prayers and presence.

As a pastor I am required to minister to many others, and some of them have great needs which require much time and attention. But I always tell my wife, "You are my number-one sheep." She always has the priority. "But if a man does not know how to manage his own household, how will he take care of the church of God" (I Timothy 3:5).

I have pointed out these scriptural goals and pray that they will serve as helpful guidelines. They are not intended to be an exhaustive list of goals but a suggested listing. There will be other goals which should be set in keeping with personal needs. It is my prayer that all of those contemplating marriage and those who are already married will see the value of having definite goals. It will enable them to achieve Kingdom living more easily.

CHAPTER V

The Husband's Headship

One of the reasons I enjoy teaching and ministering deliverance is that I know the fruits of it in my own life. The same is true when it comes to teaching family relationships and getting one's family into Kingdom living. I know what these truths have meant to me and my family. I have found something that blessed me, and I want to share it with others.

Years ago another minister had shared with me some of the things he had been learning about God's order for the family. I got into my own Bible study and soon discovered that I was not functioning as the head of my family. I began to seek the Lord for myself. I prayed, "Lord show me from Your Word what You expect of me as a husband and a father." I was not prepared for what the Lord revealed since it was so different from the way I had thought about my role in the family. However, it was ingrained in my spirit that the Bible is the guide for all I believe and practice, so I was open to what the Lord was showing me that needed to be changed.

The Bible is a mirror. When you look into a mirror, it will not lie to you but will tell you exactly what you are like. You may not like what you see, but, if you want to change, the mirror will guide you. If you have a smudge on your face, the mirror will show you where it is and when it is finally cleansed away. The way to get the mirror to do its work for you is to stay before it doing what it shows you needs to be done until you are clean and groomed. (See James 1:23-25.)

The first thing I saw was the order which God established for the family. Our God is a God of orderliness; His rule involves a Kingdom with established government. All authority is vested in Himself and in those whom He has chosen to delegate authority. The family is a part of God's Kingdom, created to serve His purposes.

Government is established for the purpose of function. If it is not set up properly, it cannot function properly. Every government must have a head whether his title be king, president, governor, mayor or something else. The husband is designated by God as a "head" of government.

> "For the husband is the head of the wife, as Christ also is the head of the church, He Himself being the Savior of the body. But as the church is subject to Christ, so also the wives ought to be to their husbands in everything" (Ephesians 5:23-24).

Is Christ the head of the church? Just as surely the husband is head of the wife. The church is not without leadership and neither is the family.

What does God expect of the one whom He has set as head over the family? This is the question that came to me when I faced the fact that, in the sight of God, I was the head of my family. I was head whether or not I wanted to be. God had designated me as head, so I needed to find out what He required, because one day I would give an account to Him. There were four basic things the Lord showed me that He required in husband headship:

Servant

In my mind I had always pictured one in authority as having everyone else serve him. I was thinking, "Now that I am head, I will prop my feet up and let my wife bring me a lemonade and the evening newspaper." My first surprise was to discover that *I am a servant to my family.* I am to be like Christ Himself, for He is the pattern of headship. Was the head of the church a servant?

60

"And Jesus called them (the twelve) to Him and said, 'You know that the rulers of the Gentiles lord it over them, and their great men hold them in subjection, tyrannizing over them. Not so shall it be among you; but whoever wishes to be great among you must be your servant, And whoever desires to be first among you must be your slave; Just as the Son of man came not to be waited on but to serve, and to give His life as a ransom for many — the price paid to set them free' " (Matthew 20:25-28, Amplified Bible).

The twelve disciples on at least one occasion debated among themselves as to which was the greatest. As they began to understand that Jesus was the Messiah and would eventually rule over the whole world, they began to jostle for position. James and John were maneuvering for positions at the right and left side of the throne. When the others found out what James and John were doing, they became jealous. Therefore, Jesus found it necessary to set them an example of headship/servitude, which is the example for all in headship.

"Jesus, knowing that the Father had given all things into His hands, and that He had come forth from God, and was going back to God, rose from supper, and laid aside His garments; and taking a towel, He girded Himself about. Then He poured water into the basin, and began to wash the disciples' feet, and to wipe them with the towel with which He was girded" (John 12:3-5).

Notice that Jesus was fully aware of who He was. He was the Son of God who had come from God and was going back to God, and the One whom the Father had placed in authority over all things. It was in full recognition of His headship that He humbled Himself and performed one of the lowliest of services. Then He gave his disciples this teaching:

"You call Me Teacher and Lord; and you are right, for so I am. If I then, the Lord and the Teacher, washed your feet, you also ought to wash one another's feet. For I gave you an example that you also should do as I did to you"

(John 13:13-15).

Once a man accepts the fact that he is a servant to his family, he must develop a servant mentality; he must think like a servant. I began to watch for opportunities to serve my wife. I discovered that it did not need to be big things but mostly many little things. There were times when she was overloaded with responsibilities and was tired in body. For example, we had just returned from a ministry trip. She was fatigued and really needed a day of rest. It was in the summer, and the produce from the garden needed to be processed. It was something that could not wait, or the vegetables would be ruined. I found an opportunity to snap beans and shell peas for canning. That might not sound like a great spiritual thing for "a man of God" to be doing, but I found that it gave me favor with the Lord and was a special blessing to my wife. I now daily try to find ways in which to demonstrate my love for my wife through deeds of thoughtfulness.

Each morning, before I get involved in my own routine of work, I ask my wife, "Is there anything that I can do for you today?" It is a security and comfort to her to know that I care about her needs. It has drawn us closer together, and I actually enjoy doing things to bless her. Being a servant has its rewards.

God expressed His wrath against the "shepherds of Israel" because they abused their headship by failure to serve their flocks. A man's family is his "flock," and his wife is his number-one-sheep.

> "Then the word of the Lord came to me saying, 'Son of man, prophesy against the shepherds of Israel. Prophesy and say to those shepherds, Thus says the Lord God, Woe, shepherds of Israel who have been feeding themselves! Should not the shepherds feed the flock?' " (Ezekiel 34:1-2).

This passage goes on to warn the shepherds who fail to minister to those who are sick, to seek those who are lost and to gather those who are scattered. Because of the shepherd's selfish concern for himself rather than for those under his headship, the sheep become prey to the beasts of the field. The beasts of the field represent the devil who is the enemy of the family, the roaring lion roaming about seeking whom he may devour. Unless a husband and father cares for his family, its members will suffer needs which will make them open game for the devil. God will hold such men accountable.

Leader

The head of the family is to be the leader. In fact, the Scripture calls him a "ruler." The first text which proves this goes back to Genesis and the Garden of Eden where God told Eve of Adam's headship over her in these words, "And he shall rule over you" (Genesis 3:16).

A second place where the husband is referred to as a ruler is in I Timothy 3:4 (King James) where the qualifications of a bishop are set forth. We need to recognize the fact that God is not setting a different standard for bishops as over against other men, but is simply emphasizing that those who are appointed to leadership in the church must first prove themselves at home. A bishop must be:

> "One who manages his own household well, keeping his children under control with all dignity (but if a man does not know how to manage his own household, how will he take care of the church of God?" (I Timothy 3:4-5).

Now, I also had my own mental picture of a ruler. I could see myself seated on a throne with a scepter in my hand, having everyone bow down before me. Do you know what a scepter is? It is a glorified stick! Since I was a ruler; after all, that is what God has designated me, then I expected those under me to do exactly what I told them to do. If they failed to respond as I desired, then I would beat them over the head with my scepter.

God said, "You have it all wrong. That is the wrong picture of a ruler." So, I looked up the word "rule" in the Greek word study book, and it completely destroyed my mental picture of a king sitting on his royal throne. The word "rule" means to stand before others as an example: to lead the way for others to follow. Paul expressed this idea accurately when, as one in headship, he challenged the Corinthian church, "Be imitators of me, just as I also am of Christ" (I Corinthians 11:1).

As a ruler then, the husband/father is to set an example for his wife and children to follow. He says in effect, "Watch me follow Christ; watch me set a Christian example, and do it like you see me do it." As a leader under God, the man has authority. However, if those under him are more aware of his power than of his helpfulness, something is wrong with his leadership methods and example.

The example of headship includes the example of submission. Jesus, the head of the church, was in complete submission to the Father. He never said or did anything except the Father gave direction. The husband must not forget that "Christ is the head of man." When a wife sees her husband fully submitted to the Lord, she will not only understand submission but will be able to submit herself to her own husband in peaceful confidence.

Lover

"Husbands, love your wives" (Ephesians 5:25). Now, this was surely something I could do well. This might be one area in which I was already overqualified as a good husband. I was always the type that liked to hug and kiss my wife. Surely I gave her plenty of love. Since I had asked the Lord to show me what He expected of me as a husband, I was ready to hear His words of approval. Instead, the Lord began to teach me the full meaning of love. I was to love my wife "as Christ also loved the church and gave himself for it."

Christ's love is a giving love and a sacrificial love. He loved us even unto death. The characteristics of Christlike love are set forth in the well-known love chapter of the Bible. Each husband needs to cultivate these truths of love until they become his nature. I have chosen to quote from the expressive language of the Amplified translation.

> "Love endures long and is patient and kind; love never is envious nor boils over with jealousy; is not boastful or vainglorious, does not display itself haughtily. It is not conceited — arrogant and inflated with pride; it is not rude (unmannerly), and does not act unbecomingly. Love [God's love in us] does not insist on its own rights or its own way, for it is not self-seeking; it is not touchy or fretful or resentful; it takes no account of the evil done to it — pays no attention to a suffered wrong. It does not rejoice at injustice and unrighteousness, but rejoices when right and truth prevail. Love bears up under anything and everything that comes, is ever ready to believe the best of every person, its hopes are fadeless under all circumstances and it endures everything [without weakening]. Love never fails — never fades out or becomes obsolete or comes to an end" (I Corinthians 13:4-8, Amplified Bible).

Between husbands and wives there can be differences in understanding the meaning of love. I remember a fine Christian woman who came to me with a complaint about her husband. She told me that her husband did not love her. She went on to explain that he had forgotten their anniversary and had not bought her a present. Furthermore, he seldom remembered her birthday or other special occasions which were to her good opportunities for him to show his love.

I wanted more evidence against the rascal, so I asked the wife what kind of provider he was. Did he hold a steady job and meet the family's financial needs? She assured me that he was a very good worker, paid all his bills and was not one to run up unnecessary debts. I asked her if he drank, gambled or ran around on her. She told me her husband was an upright man of good morals and did not do any of those things. She admitted that he was a very kind man and was never abusive to her in any way.

In this woman's mind love was a present on special occasions. To the man; love was being a good, steady provider and a faithful husband. This lady had so concentrated on what she considered to be a fault in her husband that she was unable to appreciate all of his fine qualities. I know many wives would be thankful to have such a husband as her's whether or not he remembered anniversaries or birthdays. On the other hand, this man needed to be more thoughtful about things that were of importance to his wife. This shoe fit my own foot. I saw that I was not as consistent as I should be about giving gifts to my wife.

It is out of love that a man makes provision for his wife. It was out of love that the heavenly Father made provision for our salvation. "Every good thing bestowed and every perfect gift is from above, coming down from the father of lights. . ." (James 1:17). Love manifests itself by making provision, both physical and spiritual. The physical provisions are temporal, and the spiritual provisions are eternal. I want to feed my wife with the Word of God, and I want to wash her with the water of the Word, as Jesus sanctified the church, that I might present her unto myself without spot or wrinkle or any such thing.

It is out of love that a man protects his wife. The Scripture says:

> "Just as a father has compassion on his children, So the Lord has compassion on those who fear Him. For He Himself knows our frame; He is mindful that we are but dust" (Psalm 103:13-14).

The Hebrew word "compassion" means the tenderest of loves. Because the Lord loves us so tenderly, He remembers that we are frail and need His special oversight. This is what the Scripture means when it says, "Husbands likewise, live with your wives in an understanding way, as with a weaker vessel" (I Peter 3:7).

This verse about the wife being the "weaker vessel" is another one that I had misinterpreted all my life. I thought it meant that the husband was superior to his wife. I thought it said that I was strong and she was weak. The word "weaker" is comparative rather than superlative, meaning the wife is just a little weaker than the husband is weak. It says nothing at all about the husband being strong.

I had also interpreted the word "weaker" to signify that she was inferior; and, therefore, to mean that I was superior. Once again I had read the verse incorrectly. God asked me what kind of vessels we had in our home. I told Him we had pottery, china and crystal. He asked me which of these I considered the strongest and which was the weakest. I replied that the pottery was the most durable. We could toss it in the dishwasher with little special care, but the china and crystal required special handling. Then, the Lord wanted to know which of these vessels I considered the best. Well, the china and crystal are the most expensive. The crystal is the best we have in our home. So, the Lord showed me that that is the way with my wife. The "weaker vessel" is more easily broken. Ida Mae confesses that she tends to crack easily! But she is also the best I have. She needs and deserves special care.

Steward

What does the Lord expect of a husband as the head of his family? That he be a good steward of the family God has entrusted to him. The Lord Jesus said to the Father, "All things that are mine are Thine" (John 17:10). He was referring to the twelve whom the Father had entrusted to Him. Jesus was recognizing His stewardship responsibility over these men. A man may say, "This is my family," but the truth of the matter is that the family belongs to God, and the man is set as a steward over it.

When a man recognizes that he is a steward of something

that belongs to God and that as a steward he must ultimately give an account to God for the management of those things and people that are His, it puts a whole new perspective upon being a husband and a father. Wherever God delegates authority of headship, there will be an accounting. Notice that this is true of those whom God has set in spiritual authority in the church:

> "Obey your leaders, and submit to them; for they keep watch over your souls, as those who will give an account. Let them do this with joy and not with grief, for this would be unprofitable for you" (Hebrews 13:17).

In the 17th chapter of John we find what is commonly referred to as "The High Priestly Prayer of Jesus." In this prayer Jesus is giving His account to the Father of His stewardship over the men entrusted to Him. He is ending His earthly ministry and is about ready to return to the Father, so it is time for the accounting. One day I, along with all other husbands, will give an account to God for the stewardship of the family. God will not require this of the wife and mother because she is not the head; he will not require the children to answer for the family since they are not in headship.

As we examine the prayer of Jesus by reflecting on His report to the Father, we are able to see the principles that govern all headship. By observing what Jesus did in headship over His disciples, we learn what is expected of a husband/father.

Beginning with the sixth verse of John seventeen there is found at least one principle of headship in each of the following fourteen verses. In some verses there are two or three principles. Let me share with you what the Holy Spirit revealed to me:

Principles of Headship From John 17

1. *Manifesting the Father:* "I manifested Thy name to the men"

68

(v. 6). To manifest the name of the Father is to show through one's own life the nature and character of the Heavenly Father. This is the duty of the head of the family. He is the father image. A child learns to identify with God the Father through his relationship with his earthly father. It has been proven time after time that a child who has a poor example in his earthly father is unable to identify with God as being kind, gentle, forgiving and loving.

2. *Accepting his family as a gift from God:* ". . . whom Thou gavest Me out of the world" (v. 6). A man should openly tell his family, "You are a gift from God; you are the ones whom God has entrusted to me." Everywhere I teach on family relationship, I exhort the men to do this. After I had done so at a particular conference, the next morning a man and his wife approached me hand in hand. She was beaming. She said, "My husband did exactly as you suggested. When we returned to our room last evening he took me by both hands, looked right into my eyes, and with all his heart said, 'You are a gift from God; you are the wife whom God has given me.' " She said that he had never said anything like that to her before, and she was so blessed she could not keep from grinning. Men, it may seem like a small thing, and it may be a little awkward for some of you to do, but it will be such a blessing to your family. They need to hear you say with your own mouth that they are accepted and loved by you.

Notice Jesus spoke of those who were given to him "out of the world." In other words, they were not perfect when He received them, but He still loved them and acknowledged them. When I stood at the marriage altar and said "I do" in response to the pastor's question, "Do you take the woman you hold by the right hand to be your lawful and wedded wife?" I took her just as she was. The disciples often displayed their imperfections, yet Jesus never rejected them because of it. He was always thankful for them. This is the way a man is to accept his family.

3. *Brings his own into obedience to God's Word:* "... and they have kept Thy word" (v. 6). It is the duty of the family head to bring each member of the home into obedience to God's Word. There must be instilled in their hearts an appreciation for the Word. The Word will continually be upheld as the standard by which all speech and activities are regulated. How blessed when a man is able to give the same good report to the Father that Jesus gave concerning His disciples.

4. *Functions by the wisdom and power of God:* "Now they have come to know that everything Thou hast given Me is from Thee" (v. 7). It is implied that a head will minister to his own. When a man ministers to his family, that family should be aware that he has not given to them out of his own mind and ability but with those of God. His teachings, counsel and power are from the throne of God. This means that a man must continually seek the Lord. The questions of life are too complicated and too important to ignore or to give an answer off the top of one's head. One must have the wisdom of God.

5. *Gives them the words received from God:* "... and for the words which Thou gavest Me I have given to them" (v. 8). He gave them the "rhema," the words spoken or uttered by the Father. Jesus always knew what the Father was saying because He stayed in prayer fellowship with the Father. The husband must do the same. There are many times when the family needs a fresh and direct word from the Lord about something. The head must walk in the Spirit so that he will always be able to hear and convey that word, just as Jesus did.

6. *Leads the family into faith:* "... and they received them (His Words). . . and they believed" (v. 8). Jesus led His disciples into faith in Him as Savior. A father will lead his own children to the Lord. He will not leave that blessing to a pastor or a Sunday school teacher, much less to chance.

I am ever thankful that it was my own father who led me to the Lord Jesus Christ as my personal Savior when I was ten years of age. I remember how he sat down with me in the living room and explained how Jesus died for my sins and then led me to a personal faith in Christ.

The head will also lead his own into the full life of faith: faith to receive the promises of God. Jesus is often found encouraging faith in those who sought Him and followed Him. He encouraged the twelve to exercise their own faith to feed the multitude and encouraged Peter to walk on the water. Wherever He found faith He commended it. Every head should be as "The Head," a teacher of faith.

7. *Prays for his own:* "I ask on their behalf; I do not ask on behalf of the world, but of those whom Thou has given Me" (v. 9). Jesus is not saying that He is uninterested in the world; He died for the world. He is declaring His priority in prayer for His own. Jesus would pray aloud in the presence of His disciples. The Lord has shown me what a blessing this is to my wife. Sometimes she would come to me with a prayer request, and then a few days later she would ask me if I had ever prayed about the matter. But now when she has a prayer request, I will pray out loud in her presence, and she both knows that I prayed and how I prayed. I know she is strengthened by my prayers, because I am still strengthened in my spirit by the prayers which I have heard my father pray for me.

8. *Acknowledges his stewardship:* ". . . for they are Thine; and all things that are Mine are Thine" (v. 9b-10a). In Matthew 25:14ff is found the familiar parable of the talents. The Kingdom of Heaven is compared to a man traveling into a far country who entrusted all of his goods to his servants. Upon his return he rewarded those who had been faithful. Each head of a family is such a servant entrusted with those who, in reality, belong to the Lord. The one who has ruled well his own household will hear these words: "Well done, good and faithful slave; you were faithful with a few things,

71

I will put you in charge of many things, enter into the joy of your master" (Matthew 25:21).

When Christ returns He will rule the earth. His Kingdom will have come on earth even as it is in Heaven, and those who rule well will be promoted to "rule over many things." They will also enter into the joys of the Lord. I want to be in that number! Don't you?

9. *He is honored in them:* ". . . and I have been glorified in them" (v. 10). His work is not unfruitful. He sees in them the reflection of His own glory. As a man sees the inwrought glory of Christ in the lives of his own, it becomes a glory to him; and he is honored by the very Christlikeness into which he has led them. A man's family becomes his credentials. Paul expressed it when he said:

> "You are our letter, written in our hearts, known and read by all men; being manifested that you are a letter of Christ, cared for by us, written not with ink but with the Spirit of the living God, not on tablets of stone, but on tablets of human hearts" (II Corinthians 3:2-3).

10. *Transfers headship when appropriate:* "And I am no more in the world; and yet they themselves are in the world, and I come to Thee. Holy Father, keep them in Thy name" (v. 11). Jesus was facing the cross and after that His resurrection and return to the Father. He could no longer walk with His disciples upon this earth as He had done. He transferred His headship over them back into the hands of the Father.

This principle of transferral of headship is seen again in what Jesus did for His mother. Evidently Joseph had died, and Jesus had assumed an earthly headship over Mary, His mother. While He was dying on the cross, He was not unmindful of her need for headship.

> "When Jesus therefore saw His mother, and the disciple whom He loved standing nearby, He said to His mother, 'Woman, behold your son!' Then He said to the disciple, 'Behold your mother!' And from that hour the disciple took her into his own household" (John 19:26-27).

72

Transferral of headship occurs when a daughter marries. This is what takes place when a father gives the bride in marriage. She has been under his headship since birth: but now she is being married, and the husband will be her head. When the father gives the bride away, it means that he is releasing headship over his daughter, and when the bridegroom says "I do," it means that he is assuming that headship.

11. *Leads them into union with God:* "While I was with them, I was keeping them in Thy name which Thou has given Me; and I guarded them, and not one of them perished but the son of perdition, that the Scripture might be fulfilled" (v. 12). The devil knew how strategic it was to capture the twelve disciples, and he tempted them in many ways. The world and the devil are out to capture our children and youth as never before. A father must be diligent each day if he expects to give a successful report to the Father that none have been lost to the hippies, the Moonies or the world.

12. *Maintains family joy:* "But now I come to Thee; and these things I speak in the world, that they may have My joy made full in themselves" (v. 13). Some things had come up that were threatening the joy of the disciples. Jesus had been speaking to them of His death and of His going away. He did not leave them in confusion but spoke such words that would insure the maintenance of their joy.

A man is responsible for maintaining joy in the family. When he sees anything that threatens that joy, he must speak to it. A vital part of Kingdom living is "joy in the Holy Spirit" (Romans 14:17). Many things threaten this joy, but it should never be lost.

13. *Separates them from the world:* "I have given them Thy word; and the world has hated them, because they are not of the world, even as I am not of the world" (v. 14). Unless a family is established in the Word of God, it will be over-

73

come by the world. The influence of the world is called worldliness. Worldliness is spoken of by Jesus as "the cares of life."

Young people are especially vulnerable to peer pressure: the pressure to conform to this world. They may become afraid of not being accepted by the world. Jesus knew that He had done a good job of training His disciples when He saw that the world hated them. The world cannot tolerate anything godly; the world does not like to be reminded of God. Darkness does not love the Light.

Notice that Jesus led the way in overcoming the world. The head must always set the example. We cannot expect our families to be something different from the head of that family. He must lead the way.

14. *Prays their influence be felt:* "I do not ask Thee to take them out of the world" (v. 15). When a family is functioning for the glory of God, it has great spiritual influence. It has become the light of the world and the salt of the earth. Its members are ready to go and be with the Lord, so far as personal salvation is concerned, but God has a purpose for their lives here on earth.

This prayer of Jesus also reflects His complete confidence in those whom He had trained. He knew that they could remain in the world and still not be overcome by the world. They did not have to be kept separated from the world and kept in a cloister in order to maintain spiritual victory. What a blessing when the head of the family knows that his own are able to withstand every pull of the world and remain true to Christ.

15. *Prays they be kept from the devil:* ". . . but to keep them from the evil one" (v. 15). A man should pray for the spiritual protection of his family. The devil is always roaming about seeking whom he may devour. A man cannot personally guard his family himself. No matter how hard he might try, there will always be times when he cannot be with his family personally, but the Lord can. He will pray for the watchcare

74

of the Lord Himself and have the same assurance that the Psalmist expressed:

> "For you have made the Lord my refuge, Even the Most High, your dwelling place. No evil will befall you, Nor will any plague come near your tent. For He will give His angels charge concerning you, To guard you in all your ways" Psalm 91:9-11).

16. *Sets them apart unto God:* "They are not of the world, even as I am not of the world" (v. 16). Just as Jesus was not of the world, but was set apart to do the will of the Father, so were His disciples set apart unto God. They were separated from the world in order that they might be separated unto God. This is a major goal of headship. When a man has brought his wife and children into a state of separation from the world, they are ready to be presented up to the glory of God.

17. *Prays for their sanctification:* "Sanctify them in the truth: Thy word is truth" (v. 17). Now He prays for the second feature of sanctification. Sanctification includes both cleansing and setting apart unto God. The Word of God is that which cleanses a person from the defilements of the world. In the same way that Christ sanctifies His church by the washing of the Word, the husband is to sanctify his wife.

> "Husbands, love your wives, just as Christ also loved the church and gave Himself up for her; that He might sanctify her, having cleansed her by the washing of water with the word, that He might present to Himself the church in all her glory, having no spot or wrinkle or any such thing; but that she should be holy and blameless. So husbands ought also to love their wives as their own bodies. He who loves his own wife loves himself" (Ephesians 5:25-28).

As a man reads the Word of God to his family, he prays that God will bless it to the cleansing of each member. Each home should have a family altar. The Word of God should be read and taught in the home by the father. Thus, he cleanses them by the Word.

18. *Sends them out in ministry:* "As thou didst send Me into the world, I also have sent them into the world" (v. 18). The fields are white unto harvest and in need of laborers. The objective for the family is to bring its members to maturity so it can minister for the Lord unto the world. So many people are so wrapped up in their own problems that they are unable to minister to others. Jesus here shows us that after three and a half years with His disciples, they were ready to do the work for which He had trained them.

19. *Sanctifies Himself:* "And for their sakes I sanctify Myself, that they themselves also may be sanctified in truth" (v. 19). Again, we see that it is the head who as a "ruler" stands out front to set the example for the others. Christ's own sanctification meant the cross. When He set Himself apart to do the Father's will, He laid down His life. In a man's commitment to the Lord, neither his vocation or his avocation is sacred. Everything is laid on the altar. The Lord Himself will determine the use of the vessel. Such sanctification brings one into freedom. To the natural mind it seems like bondage to be under the Lord's control; but, since that is why we were created, it is the only way to be free. There are many such paradoxes in Kingdom living.

It was "for their sakes" that He laid down His life. The calling to headship is a calling to death to self. The only way that a man can be a successful husband and father is to die to self and live to the Lord. It is a high calling.

CHAPTER VI

The Wife's Submission

As the family takes its position in the Kingdom of God, each member of that family must align him or her self as God has directed. The husband must be in the position of headship, the wife in her position of submission, and the children in their place of obedience and respect. As each one comes into Divine order, he passes through his own battles. Sometimes the battle can be very intense. The devil will discourage in every way he can. He will tell a person that it is all wrong, that it will not work, that his circumstances are different and therefore unapplicable, that he cannot change until another member changes first, that he is not strong enough, that it is not time to start or that it will take too long to finish.

It has been interesting to watch people come up against their personal challenges. At the very start, one must be convicted that Divine order and Kingdom living are scriptural and intended for him. He must make a quality decision to press through to the goal. He must know that God is with him to strengthen and guide. He must be assured in his heart, by faith, that the reward will be worth the effort.

I remember the struggles that Ida Mae and I went through to get where we are in Kingdom living as I learned to assume headship and she learned to submit. Most of the time we were able to work out areas of difficulty on our own, but a few times we had to resort to outside counsel. At times, nests of demons would be flushed up. Along with the renewing of our minds and the disciplining of our flesh, there were the essential times of spiritual warfare and deliverance.

The Kingdom of God is never established without a fight. This is the pattern throughout Scripture. Jesus came to preach the Gospel of the Kingdom, and the first thing He had to face when He began His ministry was the contest with Satan in the wilderness temptations. When Jesus returns to establish His Kingdom on earth, it will be preceded by the coming of an angel with a great chain; and the key to the bottomless pit, to bind Satan and to shut him up in the pit for a thousand years. (See Revelation 20:1-3.)

Casting out demons is necessary to gain one's position in the Kingdom. When Jesus had delivered a man from blindness and dumbness, He chose the occasion to give us this guiding principle: "But if I cast out demons by the Spirit of God, the Kingdom of God has come upon you" (Matthew 12:28). That poor man was outside the blessings of Kingdom living until he experienced deliverance.

Do you think a strong man will stand passively as we bind him? Jesus said the Kingdom is gained when we "first bind the strong man." Then we can enter that strong man's house and spoil his goods. Jesus ended this particular discourse by stating:

> "He who is not with Me is against Me; and he who does not gather with Me scatters" (Matthew 12:30).

Jesus fought and bound the devil in order to establish His Kingdom. We must align ourselves with Christ in spiritual warfare and deliverance ministry or else we have taken the devil's side in the matter! There is no alternative.

Ida Mae and I had been married twenty-five years when we launched the attack to gain Kingdom living. A lot of wrong habit patterns had been established. Before the building could begin, the bulldozer had to do its work. Tearing down old concepts and old habits can be very painful, as we discovered.

Although we worked side by side in the ministry, we functioned separately from one another. I provided no headship for her physically, mentally, emotionally or spiritually. Her health was in shambles. If she felt she needed medical help she called doctors, took medication and scheduled surgery. Her resentments, moods and griefs were all outside my right to govern. She had her own Bible study and prayer life; her spiritual functions were independent of my authority. You can well imagine that when she first heard an anointed sermon from the text: "Wives, submit yourselves unto your own husbands as unto the Lord . . . in everything," she wondered, "How in the world could I ever do that?"

When my wife made the decision to submit to me, she felt completely devastated. Her whole life was thrown suddenly into reverse gear. Demons shrieked in her ear night and day telling her that she was crazy, that I could not be depended upon, that she had a right to be in control of her own life and that she might as well die.

When my wife finally told me that she was now willing for me to make decisions and seek God in her behalf, I became extremely fearful of the responsibility. I had always been able to get her to make my decisions for me, and I had come to depend upon her to make important family decisions; because I had always been so indecisive about everything. I would not let myself believe that she had really submitted herself to me. I would test her by asking, "What do you think we should do about so-and-so?" To my horror she developed a stock answer: "You decide, and when you tell me then we will both know." This drove me to my knees in a hurry. I had to have help, and the only help available was God. As it turned out, this is the best thing that could have happened to me. God did not fail me.

If you do not think arriving at Kingdom living involves a fight, just make a solid decision to obey God's Word for what it says, and the devil will immediately throw at you every doubt, fear and accusation in his arsenal.

We have spoken earlier about the Kingdom of God being equated with rule, authority and government, but we must not forget that it is also equated with love. The same thing can be said about authority without love as is said about spiritual gifts without love: "It profits me nothing" (I Corinthians 13:3). A man can have authority, but if he has no love he will be harsh, cruel, selfish and unfair. If he has love and no authority, he is like a jellyfish. He has the compassion and desire to bless, but there is no ability for love to do its work. Love needs a backbone.

God is love. He has proven His love for us over and over again. He has authority over our lives, and it is easy to submit to God's authority by recognizing His infinite love. The authority which God has delegated to a husband must be administered in love. "Husbands, love your wives . . ." is not a Divine suggestion but a command. My love is the thing that made submission palatable for my wife, and it will do the same for others.

Understanding Submission

"Wives, be subject to your own husbands, as to the Lord . . . as the church is subject to Christ, so also the wives ought to be to their husbands in everything" (Ephesians 5:22,24).

In recent years much has been said and written about the wife's submission. Some of it has been unbalanced. I have found women prone to be defensive when the subject is broached. When I teach on this subject, I find it necessary to break down some barriers first. A woman can be so prejudiced against submission that she will be spiritually deaf: unable to hear the Word of the Lord.

Although some teaching on submission may be unbalanced and unfair, God's Word is neither unbalanced or unfair. God does not hate women and neither did the Apostle Paul! When a woman understands scriptural submission, she will appreciate God's love for her. God's love has placed the wife in a position of special protection. He has a purpose for her to fulfill for His glory which cannot be fulfilled if she is not in her rightful position of submission. Her family can never be brought into Kingdom living without her submission, for the family cannot come into Divine order if the wife is out of position.

Let it be clearly understood that the wife is of equal importance but of different function. A wife's submission does not make her a second-class citizen in God's Kingdom. Submission does not determine a wife's worth but her function. In the sight of God the husband and wife are of equal importance. They do not each have to fulfill the same functions in order to be of equal importance. A woman does not have to be in leadership to be important. That is worldly philosophy.

The following Scriptures teach us that husband and wife are of equal importance to God:

> "However, in the Lord, neither is woman independent of man, nor is man independent of woman. For as the woman originates from the man, so also the man has his birth through the woman; and all things originate from God" (I Corinthians 11:11-12).

> "You husbands, likewise, live with your wives in an understanding way, as with a weaker vessel since she is a woman; and grant her honor as a fellow heir of the grace of life, so that your prayers may not be hindered" (I Peter 3:7).

> "For you are all sons of God through faith in Christ Jesus . . . There is neither Jew nor Greek, there is neither slave nor free man, there is neither male nor female; for you are all one in Christ Jesus" (Galatians 3:26-28).

It is a mistake to interpret these passages to mean that since the husband and wife, man and woman, are equal in the benefits of God's grace that it follows that they are the same in function. Only as a man is functioning in the Lord in headship is he able to fulfill God's calling upon his life. Likewise, only as a woman is functioning in the Lord in submission is she able to fulfill God's calling upon her life. If

81

the roles are confused, the purposes of God are confused.

Furthermore, the Scripture is consistent on the position of the woman's submission, whether it be in the family or in the church.

> "Let a woman quietly receive instruction with entire submissiveness. But I do not allow a woman to teach or exercise authority over a man, but to remain quiet. For it was Adam who was first created, and then Eve. And it was not Adam who was deceived, but the woman being quite deceived, fell into transgression" (I Timothy 2:11-14).

It would be utter confusion if the man were head at home and the woman head in the church. The above Scripture sets forth two reasons why God made the man head. First, Adam was formed and then Eve. Man's headship follows the natural order of creation. God saw that it was not good for man to be alone, and Eve was created as a completing for Adam, that is as a helpmeet. Second, it was the woman who was deceived rather than the man. God knows woman, for He has created her. It is God who refers to her as the "weaker vessel." He knows her proneness to deception, so He has graciously placed her under the covering of her husband for the sake of protection.

There are three principle texts in the New Testament which set forth the submission of the wife to her husband: Ephesians 5:22-24, Colossians 3:18 and I Peter 3:1. In each of these texts, the wife's submission is mentioned before anything at all is addressed to the husband. To the natural mind this order seems reversed. Why not speak to the "head" first? For the simple reason that a man cannot lead until he has a follower. This means that the wife has a key function in getting the family into Divine order. She has not been given the authority of leadership, but she has been given a place of great influence.

The word translated "submission" or "subjection" in the King James translation is "hupotasso." Whenever this word is used in reference to the wife's submission, it is always in the middle voice in the Greek construction. It is to be literally translated "submit yourself." There is no such thing as forced submission. A husband cannot force his wife to submit to him, for that would amount to control. God condemns control and tyranny. Submission is a completely voluntary act on the part of the wife.

"Hupotasso" is a military term. One of the Greek lexicons gives this definition: "to set in array, as a soldier under a commanding officer." When I saw this definition, I got a picture of the First Sergeant who was over me in the army. He had been written up in *Life Magazine* as "the toughest top kick in the United States Army," and he certainly lived up to his reputation. Was the wife to be one who simply took orders from a gruff, insensitive husband who functioned like a First Sergeant? No, indeed! "Hupotasso" emphasizes setting in array: to arrange in an orderly fashion as a rank of soldiers. The purpose of soldiers being set in rank is function. If a company of soldiers had no leadership on the battlefield, the result would be chaos. There must be a leader and the rest followers. The family IS in warfare as we have already pointed out, but it cannot expect victory unless it is set in array. What is the opposite of array? It is disarray. A family with an unsubmissive wife is in disarray!

Jesus Himself, as our pattern of submission, was set in array. In His humanity He humbled Himself and submitted Himself to the Father. Was Jesus God? Yes, indeed. Was He equal with God? Yes, indeed. Did He have a different function to fulfill than the Father's? Yes, indeed. Can you see that Jesus could be in submission without being inferior? This stopped Satan in his tracks. A verse which speaks of Christ's triumph over Satan is followed by a verse which speaks of His obedient submission to the Father:

> "I will not speak much more with you, for the ruler of the world is coming, and he has nothing in Me; but that the world may know that I love the Father, and as the Father gave Me commandment, even so I do" (John

14:30-31).

Notice that our text in Ephesians 5:22 says a wife is told to submit to her own husband, not to every man. Again, it leads to confusion if a woman attempts to submit to more than one man. In effect, she has more than one head and the chances are they will be in conflict. This is one reason why I think it should be a prayer goal for each family that the wife not have to work outside the family.

A man that I know felt it was necessary for his wife to supplement the family income by finding a job. She finally obtained what looked like the ideal position: working as a church secretary. At least she would be working for a spiritual man and contributing directly to the work of the Lord. Shortly after she took the job, at the close of the Sunday morning service, her husband spoke to her that they needed to get home because he was hungry, and she needed to prepare lunch. About that time the pastor stepped up and told her that he needed her to stay for an extra hour and do some work for him in the office. Even in the best of situations, it is nothing less than confusing if a woman is trying to submit to two different men. Such a wife is forced to choose between submitting to her husband or to another man. We can immediately see the wisdom of God in saying, "Wives submit yourselves unto your own husbands."

Whenever I counsel or minister deliverance to a married woman, I remember that she has husband headship. If at all possible, I prefer to have the husband present when I minister to the wife. I like for him to lay hands on her, pray for her and command evil spirits out of her. There is one thing for sure: the devil does not like to see a husband take that responsibility for his wife. There is always a greater anointing for deliverance when the wife's God-appointed head is functioning. If the husband is not available for some reason, then I am careful not to override his authority. He is still her head even if he is not following the Lord and is not present for her ministry.

As to the Lord

What does it mean that the wives are to submit to their husbands "as to the Lord?" This is the facet of submission that lifts it from the natural plane to the spiritual. Since the husband bears God's delegated authority, the way a wife acknowledges and honors God's authority is through her submission. Through submission to her husband the wife obeys, serves and submits to God. A wife may chafe under submission by thinking that God only approves of her if the husband is totally right in everything he does. However, God approves of the wife who submits to the authority which He has placed in the family.

It is easy for the wife to get her eyes upon the faults of her husband rather than upon obedience to God, particularly if the husband is weak in headship or is harsh and unfair in his administration of headship. If she concentrates on the husband's failures, she will fall into rebellion against him or will initiate various attempts to sanctify him.

The wife must avoid these pitfalls to submission. She must not assume responsibility for her husband's shortcomings. "Christ is the head of man." Christ is responsible for the husband's sanctification. The best thing for a wife to do is to pray for her husband and place him in the Lord's hands. She needs to be completely honest with the Lord in her prayers. If she entered into marriage without consulting God's will, she needs to confess this sin. If she was a believer and married an unbeliever, she should confess the sin of disobedience to God's counsel that she not be unequally yoked together with an unbeliever. If she has complicated the marriage relationship through wrong words, actions or attitudes, she should confess this to God and to her husband. If she is reaping what she has sown, she must pray for God's mercy.

A turning point in relationship between my wife and me came when she truly submitted herself to my headship and began to pray for me. She had to break a bad habit of telling

God all my faults and to start praying for me in a positive way. From her point of view, this new way of praying gave her a vision of what God could do, and her words and attitudes began to nurture the vision of a better husband. She laid down the heavy responsibility for my reform, and put it all in the hands of God. Her frustration with God over not doing something about her problem with her husband was replaced by faith that God *was* doing something. She had placed herself in a position to be used of God in answering her own prayers!

From my point of view, I was placed in a completely new position. I no longer felt the pressures of my wife's rebellion or of her attempts to reform me. I found myself desiring to be a good head over my wife, and I could do it with my own initiative. This was not an overnight change in me or in her. There were times when each of us lapsed into our old habit patterns. But we had established communication; we were seeking a fuller understanding of God's Word and we were each in prayer desiring God's strength.

A wife cannot force her husband to be a strong and good head over her anymore than a husband can force his wife to submit to him. Each must get out of the way and let God do His work. Each must stand in faith for God to do what the other is unable to do himself. The Bible teaches that genuine faith is characterized by a patience that endures. Patience is of the essence in working out relationships. It keeps us from giving up or blowing up when nothing seems to be happening.

Since the wife is dependent upon the Lord to function as head over her husband, she must be patient with the Lord as she stands in obedience. I wish to point out that it is not sufficient to stand in faith and not also stand in obedience. There are conditions for the wife to meet before she can expect God's help. If she is not in submission to her husband, then she is not waiting on God but God is waiting on her.

But how can she be submissive to an imperfect husband? Only "as to the Lord." The Lord is perfect, and all His ways are perfect. The Lord requires her submission so that she will submit to her husband in obedience to the Lord. She will submit in the knowledge that submission to her husband is, in reality, submission to the Lord and that failure to submit to her husband is rebellion against God. She will understand from God's Word that submission to her husband gains approval from God and puts her in a position to be blessed of God.

The principle of submission does not vary, but remains the same whether the submission is of a wife to her husband or a citizen to those in civil authority. Since it is required of God, one cannot ignore submission without opposing God's ordinance and incurring God's judgment.

> "Let every person be in subjection to the governing authorities. For there is no authority except from God, and those which exist are established by God. Therefore he who resists authority has opposed the ordinance of God; and they who have opposed will receive condemnation upon themselves" (Romans 13:1-2).

Obedience to God is essential to maintaining a good conscience, maintaining a good conscience is essential to faith, and faith is essential to answered prayer.

> "Wherefore it is necessary to be in subjection, not only because of wrath, but also for conscience's sake" (Romans 13:5).

> "Beloved, if our heart does not condemn us, we have confidence before God: and whatever we ask we receive from Him, because we keep His commandments and do the things that are pleasing in His sight" (I John 3:21-22).

In Everything

> "But as the church is subject to Christ, so also the wives ought to be to their husbands in everything" (Ephesians 5:24).

If only the Word had not said "in everything." Is that not the way most wives feel about it? That phrase "in every-

87

thing" closes up all the loopholes to submission. It prevents a wife from excusing herself from submission if she thinks her husband is exercising poor judgment or acting in a bad spirit. It means that a wife cannot lightly excuse herself from submission by claiming exceptions to the husband's authority.

Headship means little unless submission is complete. A wife may submit surface matters without submitting root matters. Partial obedience is tantamount to disobedience and partial submission is tantamount to rebellion.

There was a point in my wife's submitting to me that I felt she had truly submitted everything. I was not aware of anything that was not submitted. So, it was a surprise when she approached me one day to confess that there was an area of her life that remained unsubmitted. She said that she had never submitted her private thoughts and opinions, and she wanted me to sanctify her in these areas, but she had some deep fears about submitting such personal and tender areas of her being.

Before Ida Mae could submit these areas which she had reserved just for herself, she needed my assurance that I would handle the matter rightly. Because of previous hurts, she wanted to be sure that I would not laugh at her, scold her or ignore her. By submitting other areas of her life to me, she had gained partial confidence in my headship and had more assurance of my love.

Within myself I thought I was now fully prepared to accept headship over anything my wife submitted to me. I assured her that I could handle whatever she needed to disclose. As she began to share with me her innermost being, I was shocked. I began to say things like, "You surely don't feel that way . . . How in the world could you think that? . . . You shouldn't think that way." Then I remembered my commitment to handle it right, and I began to pray for God's wisdom to shoulder this new responsibility.

This step of submission on Ida Mae's part was necessary for us to become truly "one in the Lord." All the roots were exposed and submitted. She had become transparent, and I had become responsible. It makes it much easier for a wife to submit when her husband meets her with responsible love. A wife cannot, however, require a good attitude on the part of her husband as a condition for submission. If a husband wants a submissive wife, then he should give her such understanding love that she will not be afraid to share with him the secrets of her heart.

The question then comes, "What if the husband expects the wife to submit to something sinful?" Suppose he wants her to go to the bar with him to drink, to attend x-rated movies or become involved in wife swapping? Does the Scripture requiring the wife to submit to her husband "in everything" include sin? It is my conviction that this is where the line is drawn. God does not require anyone to submit to sin. However, this does not justify rebellion on the part of the wife. Rebellion is also sin. Her refusal to submit must not be out of rebellion but out of conviction before the Lord. She may not be able to obey her husband's wishes, but she dare not become disrespectful.

A good example of this principle at work is found in the fourth chapter of Acts. In obedience to the Lord's command, the disciples were proclaiming the Gospel. The high priest and others in spiritual authority summoned the disciples and commanded them not to speak or teach in the name of Jesus. For the disciples to stop preaching would be to disobey the command of their Lord. They must obey the Lord without becoming disrespectful and rebellious against human authority. Peter addressed the priests with honor as "rulers and elders," explained why they must continue to do what they were doing, asked them to judge in the sight of God whether their request should be obeyed, and prayed for God's intervention on their behalf.

In like manner, should the husband require his wife to go against her conscience or disobey the Lord, the wife should be ready to give an answer for her faith. She must convey to her husband that she still recognizes him as her head but cannot sin against God. Then she must leave the matter in the hands of God and be prepared to face whatever consequences might follow.

The disciples kept on preaching the Gospel. Peter was put in prison, Stephen was stoned to death and James was executed with a sword. Some indeed suffered and lost their lives, but they gained eternal rewards. In speaking to servants and wives who suffer through submission the Scripture says:

> "For you have been called for this purpose. Since Christ also suffered for you, leaving you an example for you to follow in His steps, who committed no sin, nor was any deceit found in His mouth; and while being reviled, He did not revile in return; while suffering, He uttered no threats, but kept entrusting Himself to Him who judges righteously" (I Peter 2:21-23).

CHAPTER VII

The Wife's Sanctification

By Ida Mae

Soon after receiving the baptism in the Holy Spirit in 1968, we began to hear teachings and read articles on God's order for the family. This included the husband and father's headship, the wife's submission to her husband and the children's respect, obedience and honor to their parents.

I was hearing principles of headship that were never taught by my parents: principles never required of them by God or the church, although these principles have always been the core of God's Kingdom government. For all practical purposes they were not practiced in Christian homes. Now, however, God is insisting that these principles be restored, and so it was inevitable that He require Frank and me to implement them in our home relationship.

From childhood, I had been taught to read and respect the Word of God, so I was eager to be obedient to these old truths that were being restored to the Body of Christ. I agreed wholeheartedly with it all and was sincere in my efforts at obeying and implementing them in my life.

However, I thought agreeing was the same as doing. Therefore, I became very smug and prideful that I was doing the Word, because I agreed with the Word. This led me to approach God in a very boastful manner.

One day, as I was washing dishes, I was fellowshipping with God in my spirit-man. I was thinking on submission and how some women were having such a hard time with it. In my pride I said to the Lord, "How am I doing, Lord?" I fully expected Him to smile and say He was very proud of me. To my surprise He answered very firmly, "Not too well."

One should never ask God a question unless he wants an honest answer. His honesty caught me completely off guard. After getting over the initial shock, I asked Him very weakly, "What do you mean, Lord?" It was then He instructed me to get my Bible and turn to Ephesians 5:22-33. In a few minutes He gave me a revelation truth on sanctification that has taken me years to walk out in my life. The fruits of it have been unbelievably satisfying.

Satan is attacking families today as never before. Divorce, adultery, drugs, babies out of wedlock, financial pressure, cults, occult, shacking-up, alcohol, pornography, incest, molestation, homosexuality, lesbianism are just some of his devices. On and on the list goes of the heinous things the enemy uses to torment and destroy family life.

For any family to remain unscathed today by these prevalent evils, the home must be structured according to God's Divine order. Righteousness in family units must be established, and a strong guard made operative against evil. God has not been caught unaware or asleep on the job nor been overpowered by Satan.

I would like to share with you the principle of God's order for the wife's sanctification. I will give it to you just as I received it from the Spirit.

First of all, in Ephesians 5:22, the teaching begins by addressing the wives. "Wives, be subject to your own husbands, as to the Lord." Though the greater responsibility of the following verses rests on the husbands, the first appeal is to the wives. The reason for this is that a husband can do nothing with his wife until she, of her own need and desire, submits to him. Submission is truly the way of peace. This is more than a one-time decision of the will on the wife's part, rather it is a daily decision and action of her will. To intensify it even further, it is a happening to happening action. Every situation that arises in the home calls for a fresh decision of submission.

This verse also says, "be subject to your own husband." More often than not, a wife will be seeking sanctification everywhere except from her own husband. Independence, which is so deeply ingrained in women today, causes them to look to themselves for their sanctification, or choose counselors other than husbands. As we will see later, this is not God's order. No other man or woman is to sanctify a wife be it pastor, professional counselor or the next door neighbor.

The last part of that verse says, "as to the Lord." This brings us to the motivation. We submit to our own husbands because the Lord has given the pattern to follow. It has nothing to do with our opinions of our husbands' capability or qualifications, but because it is ordered by God. Obedience to the Lord is the motivating factor. Do not expect to gain any points with God if the attitude is bad. A wife with a bad attitude might say, "All right husband, I'll submit to you, not because I think you are right or deserve it, but because God said I had to." Rather, verse 33 says, "and let the wife see to it that she respect her husband."

It is contrary to God's order for a pastor, or any spiritual leader, to attempt to directly straighten out a wife apart from her husband. Not even the pastor's wife has the authority, only the wife's own husband. If the wife has some need which the husband is having difficulty with, he can seek outside help; but he should go with her for the counseling. After all, it is still his responsibility to judge the counseling; and, if the counseling is acceptable to him, he still must see to it that it is acted upon by his wife.

Wives, I want you to notice that this verse makes no exceptions. It does not say if he is a Christian, or if he is a mature Spirit-filled Christian, or if he is kind, or if this or if that. It simply says the husband is the head of the wife.

The next part of the verse tells how much, in the eyes of God, the husband really is the head, "as Christ also is the head of the church." Whether the church has submitted to Christ's headship or not, does not minimize the fact of His headship. The last part of the verse says: "He Himself being the Savior of the body." That word *Savior* means "deliverer" or "preserver." Whether the husband is functioning as a head is not the question here. The fact is that in God's family plan, the husband is the head, and he is the savior, deliverer and preserver of the body given him, namely his wife.

Because of this, and this is very important for wives to know, because man has been created in God's Divine order to be head of his wife; he has built into his nature the drive to sanctify his wife. Whether or not he is doing a good job or a bad job is not the issue. The issue is that he is placed over his wife by God and it is to that position that we wives are to submit ourselves.

Verse 24 says, "But as the church is subject to Christ, so also the wives ought to be to their husbands in everything." Too many wives put the emphasis on what "everything" excludes rather than what it includes. We wives do not submit to sin. Sin is excluded. Where you might have an occasion to exclude one sin you will have one hundred occasions to include many of the "everythings." Just because you may have to exclude sin, does not mean that you exclude "everything" along with it.

Verse 25 is addressed to the husbands. "Husbands love your wives, just as Christ also loved the church and gave Himself up for her." Now let's take the phrase "just as Christ." This phrase draws a comparison. Christ's love and care for the church is the pattern and example given for the husband's headship over his wife. When I got to this phrase "just as Christ" the Spirit said, "Insert your husband's name since the same pattern is for him."

I read verses 25-26 like this: "that Frank might sanctify me, having cleansed me by the washing of water with the Word, that Frank might present to himself his wife in all her glory, having no spot or wrinkle or any such thing but that she should be holy and blameless."

Wives, it is not our place to judge our husband's love.

It is true that if a husband deals with his wife in love it makes sanctification a lot more enjoyable. However, love is multifaceted. The Bible says, "God is love," yet in Romans 11:22 we read, "Behold then the kindness and severity of God." I will talk more about this later.

At this point the Spirit gave a very firm word. He said, "American women have this all turned around. They work diligently sanctifying their husbands so they can present their husbands to themselves having no spot or wrinkle, holy and blameless."

In my mind I saw a Christian wife holding her husband by his arm as she was taking him to the prayer group, to church and conventions and presenting him to all her friends. "See what a good job I've done," she would say. "I have him reading the Bible and praying now and then. The finances are straightened out, his clothes are coordinated; I've improved his driving abilities. I've been faithful to have everyone pray for him, and faithful to seek counsel on how to handle him. I present him to you almost spotless and blameless." Ladies, wives, you know we are all much too guilty of that. We have our little conniving ways such as nag, cry, run off, withhold bedroom privileges, pout, put tracts by the bed and in the bathroom, play tapes really loudly when he's in the house, threaten divorce: the list is endless.

I was then reminded of I Corinthians 11:3, "But I want you to understand that Christ is the head of every man, and the man is the head of a woman, and God is the head of Christ." For the first time I saw the implications in the order of that verse. Whatever a wife thinks about her husband, she thinks the same about Christ who is her husband's head, and she thinks the same about God who is Christ's head.

Respect starts from the bottom and moves upward. The wife is at the bottom. When she has respect for her husband's headship, she is having respect for Christ and God. On the other hand, when she has disrespect for her husband's headship she also has disrespect for Christ and God.

No wonder the Scripture says in Ephesians 5:33, " . . . and let the wife see to it that she respect her husband." She is not to ignore him but to respect and honor him. I personally believe a wife cannot have a clean respect for Christ and God if she has a breakdown in respect for her husband, although many a husband has given his wife reasons to feel that he does not deserve honor and respect.

Too long our thinking has been from the top down. A wife thinks that if she respects and loves Jesus and God, it does not matter what her attitude is toward her husband. God judges it in a different light. When we wives are extolling and honoring Jesus and God, I believe He receives it in the light of how we are extolling and honoring our husband's headship. I have had a much cleaner relationship with Jesus and God since I saw this truth. Can a fountain spew forth both bitter and sweet? I can not spew bitter words upon my husband and out of the same spirit speak sweet words to Jesus and God. When I harbor or speak resentment to my husband, my communication to Jesus and God is the same. It all comes from the same fountain. When I repent toward my husband and exchange the bitter water for sweet words of thankfulness and edification, I then have the same communication with Jesus and God.

The Spirit then said to me, "You are to sit down every morning and let Frank read the Word to you and he, under My direction, will sanctify you." When Frank came home, I shared what I had received. He had never seen those verses in that light before. After prayerful consideration, he accepted his responsibility and our adventure began.

We had no way of knowing what a transformation this would make in our lives. I can give it to you in a complete picture now, but then we could not even know what to anticipate. We had no idea of the intense diligence Jesus would require of us until the principle had become implemented in our lives. Ecclesiastes 7:8 says, "The end of a matter is better than its beginning." While sanctification is a daily ongoing matter and never ends as long as we are in our carnal bodies, the end to getting the principle working did finally come.

It was not until after working diligently for two years that we saw what Jesus was after. He brought us from harmony to unity! Ephesians 5:31; "For this cause a man shall leave his father and mother, and shall cleave to his wife; and the two shall become one flesh." That means unity of body, soul and spirit.

What do I mean "from harmony to unity?" By harmony I mean that for twenty-five years we had learned ways of adjusting and adapting to each other's temperaments. We never threw pots and pans or dishes at each other. We never lashed out at each other in long, verbal barrages. We did suppress a lot of resentments and bitternesses through non-communication. We had mastered the art of walking around each other's weaknesses. When I pouted he never probed me for why's. We had stressful patience to wait for each other to regain his "old self" again. I had my opinions and ways of seeing things; and he had his, and never the twain did meet.

We called it harmony because we could have a cold war going on between us but get it together enough to make a good showing by the time we arrived at church. We called it harmony; God called it hypocrisy. *The Random House Dictionary* gives this definition of hypocrisy: "A pretense of having desirable or publicly approved attitudes, beliefs, and principles that one does not actually possess." My, my, no wonder God moved in on my sanctification. I was a great pretender: smile real big and often and no one will ever see the real me inside. Psalm 55:21 says, "his mouth was smoother than butter, But his heart was war. . . ."

Now about unity. *The Random House Dictionary* gives this definition: "1. The state or quality of being one. 2. The state of being combined with others to form a greater whole. 3. Harmony or agreement. 4. Complete accord among persons regarding attitudes, opinions, intentions, etc." We were brought from harmony to unity through sanctification by the washing of water with the Word.

The first thing we did was study the word "sanctification." We found it to mean "to make holy, to set apart." It is to make inwardly whole, the putting off of sin and the putting on of holiness. It is a process of growth, bringing us to an ideal completion — that of conforming to the image of God.

Sanctification is not a garment to be put on such as a garment of righteousness but a spiritual principle for cleansing the inward man, dealing with the roots in one's life. "If the root be holy, so are the branches. . . " and "it is not you who supports the root, but the root supports you" (Romans 11;16, 18).

So, basically, the principle of sanctification is dealing with the roots in one's life whether they be good or bad. The principle of the wife's sanctification is that her husband, under the guidance of the Holy Spirit, takes the Word of God and makes whole the roots to her spirit, soul and body.

Frank did not know that scripturally he was expected to, or had a right to invade the privacy of my personal self and bring it to sanctification or wholeness and conformity to the image of God.

Hindrances Overcome

Though both of us now saw the principle of sanctification and desired to put it in operation, there were some hindrances that had to be worked through before it was working smoothly.

The first hindrance was my *independence* in the study of the Word of God. Frank, being a minister, was always much in the Word. I, too, fed often on the Word but we had never studied the Word together. We had missed totally studying the Word together in our twenty-five years of married life. The first thing Frank saw was that he was to take the leadership in selecting passages to study and deciding when and where we would study or read together.

Right off, I didn't like his first selection. I think it was Proverbs. Proverbs contains little short sayings, and I wanted something more continuous. It was our first encounter with his standing up and being the leader. He looked at me over the top of his glasses and said, "Who is sanctifying whom? We will read the Proverbs." I submitted; and we read Proverbs. It may seem like a small matter but it was a start. Frank's words became a proverb around our house and still is: "Who is sanctifying whom?"

Another hindrance was *husband intimidation.* For so many years I had intimidated my husband by my bad reactions to his attempts at correcting me that now he was fearful of stirring up more unpleasantness. I now knew that I needed help, and desired that he move in stronger on some of my weak areas, but he was hesitant, even though he now knew it was his spiritual responsibility.

Some wives, even as I did, have their husbands intimidated. Most husbands desire to live with their wives in peace, and do not like for them to "make waves." When a husband attempts to touch certain areas in his wife, if she reacts negatively he may back off in fear of stirring up unpleasantness. So, if the wife is to receive sanctification through her husband she must cease intimidating him.

To overcome this on my part, the Lord gave me the illustration of Queen Esther. Before Esther went before the king, she spent six months with oil and six months with spices. She was preparing her flesh. Anywhere the king touched her skin it would be soft, pliable and perfumed. The Lord said that is the way he wanted my flesh nature to be. Anywhere that Frank wanted to touch me, it should be soft, pliable and even perfumed. It should be a joy for him to touch my flesh. That took a bit of doing, but I was determined: so I began to work on my flesh.

A third hindrance was *husband-frustration.* For twenty-five years we had walked in our own ways. Many times he had made suggestions to me, and I had met them with indifference and insincerity. I had my own ideas, and he had his. I went my way and he went his. So, he became frustrated. Through our counseling ministry we have found many husbands who are frustrated. For example, we were once counseling a couple, and, as we gave the wife the counsel of the Lord, we could hear the husband mumbling to himself as though to say, "I have been trying to tell you that all along, but you wouldn't listen to me." She was receiving counsel from us which she would never receive from him.

The fourth hindrance was *defensiveness* and *sensitiveness when corrected.* Let's face it, most of us wives are sensitive. We do not take things like men are able to take them. We have a different nature than men, and we cannot take things emotionally as well as they usually can: therefore, we become defensive. When our husbands mention some weakness in us, we immediately want to defend it. We must mature in our emotions so that we can get past being sensitive and defensive. We must mature past the tears. Most men are very frustrated by the wife's tears, and usually react too strongly or too weakly, and this definitely hinders good communication which is necessary for good sanctification.

Deafness was the fifth hindrance. We can be deaf at convenient times. The husband says something and somehow we never hear it. We have a way of tuning out, because we do not want to hear it. We do not realize that what he is saying is really that important. We can become so opinionated that we readily dismiss our husband's input. It takes a good listener to receive good sanctification.

Disrespect was another hindrance to my sanctification. Isn't it interesting that we would have disrespect for our husbands? We develop disrespect from hurts, disappointments, resentments, rejection, conflicts, pride and many other things.

How does a wife know if she has disrespect for her husband? She feels he is not capable of sanctifying her, that he has the problems rather than herself and that he is too weak or too strong in handling her. There is a feeling that anyone except the husband can minister to her. Yet the husband is the very one whom God has ordained to sanctify the wife, and the wife has let the enemy come in and build disrespect for him; therefore, she cannot receive from him.

Scripturally and ideally a wife should not have to bypass her husband's headship to receive her sanctification. The primary reason for her looking to outsiders is her basic, unscriptural disrespect. She may feel that she is justified in her position for a variety of reasons, but she is missing God's wisdom in the matter.

Disrespect causes a wife to concentrate on her husband's weaknesses rather than trust in God to work in her behalf regardless of her husband's abilities. A continual attitude of disrespect keeps the wife in a negative, pessimistic attitude rather than in one of faith in God's ability to work in her behalf. The wife's disrespect for her husband is undoubtedly the biggest hindrance of all to the sanctification of the wife by her husband.

The seventh hindrance to my sanctification was *communication breakdown.* Since I was raised in a family in which my mother and father did not communicate, I never learned the importance of communication. When I married I discovered that communication was very important to my husband, but I had never had an example set before me. This was a serious hindrance to our relationship with one another until I became an adequate communicator. I had to purpose in my will to talk with my husband about anything and everything, although most of the time it still seemed nonessential. However, this ability to communicate became the foundation for my sanctification through my husband.

Without good communication it would be most difficult, if not impossible, to receive one's sanctification. How can a husband know your innermost needs unless you express them? Otherwise it would be a guessing game. Communication took us to the roots of my needs. Remember the Scripture I referred to earlier in Romans 11:16: "If the root be holy, so are the branches."

It is futile to sanctify the branches or surface things if you do not get back to the root cause which gives life to the branches. This can only be done with honest and good communication along with prayer and the Word of God.

You may have some or all of these hindrances or you may have others that I have failed to mention. Whatever they are, determine to conquer them and not let them be a stumbling block to your sanctification.

Things With Which We Dealt

Now, let me show you in a practical way how my sanctification progressed. Remember the Scripture says my husband is to wash me with the water of the Word. First, Frank chose the best time for us to have quiet time together. It was early in the morning before the activities of the day started. We had to rise a little earlier and really discipline our time. We would unplug the phone so there would be no interruptions. He would select a book from the Bible and read it aloud to me a chapter or two per day. Since it was for my sanctification, his primary thought was my comprehension of what was read and he selected truth that related to me personally.

The peace and satisfaction I received was a pleasant surprise. Since Christ is the head of man, He was leading Frank in a beautiful way. In essence my sanctification was from Jesus by the Holy Spirit through Frank. It was first class!

I want to share with you some of the things we dealt with, and maybe you can profit from our experience.

Underlying Bitterness

First, we dealt with underlying bitternesses. I call them underlying because many things that happen on the surface are rooted in one or more of such bitternesses. The surface conflict may not resemble the root; and, therefore, makes it more difficult to identify the root from which it comes. This was true in my own life.

Hebrews 12:15 says, "See to it that no one comes short of the grace of God; that no root of bitterness springing up causes trouble, and by it many be defiled."

Anyone who has done much counseling will readily recognize three root problems that are present in every marriage to one degree or another:

1. Things rooted in family life before marriage

2. Sexual relations

3. Money

Let us take first the things rooted in family life before marriage. We are all products of our home life as children and youth. No one comes from a perfect home setting. We acquire negative and positive personality traits according to how we related to our home environment. These personality traits go with us right into marriage. The positive traits make good building blocks for the new marriage, but the negative traits become stones of stumbling. If they are not dealt with properly they become " . . . a root of bitterness springing up causing trouble, and by it many are defiled" (Hebrews 12:15).

Next, consider the matter of sexual relationships. The saying is really true, "As it goes in the bedroom so it goes in the rest of the house." Bedroom happiness or unhappiness permeates all of life. If it doesn't go right in the bedroom it will not go right anywhere else.

Poor sexual relationships between husband and wife can have a many-faceted root. The problems could go back to sexual abuse in childhood: either fondling or molestation or outright incest. Sexual abuse in childhood leaves deep, deep, personality wounds that handicap good sexual relations in marriage.

Other roots to poor sexual relationships in marriage can

103

be sexual permiscuousness and perverseness before marriage which have left a person guilt-ridden. Then after marriage, roots of bitterness can be created by adultery, the requirement of oral sex and various sexual incompatabilities.

The last bitter root is money and the handling of the finances. I shall never, ever forget the morning this root was exposed in our Bible reading. For several mornings we had been reading through the book of James. This particular morning we started the fourth chapter, verse one: "What is the source of quarrels and conflicts among you? Is not the source your pleasures that wage war in your members?"

As Frank read that verse, the Holy Spirit put his finger on a strong root in me, and a ferocious war went off inside me: the war relating to money and finances. He continued to read, "You lust and do not have; so you commit murder. And you are envious and cannot obtain; so you fight and quarrel. You do not have because you do not ask" (James 4:2-3).

By this time I knew that Frank cannot help me unless I let him know what is going on inside. This particular washing in the Word took about three hours as we, with the help of the Holy Spirit, patiently uncovered a very sore spot in our relationship. Frank notified the office that he would not be in that morning. God showed us how to bring healing though it took several months to work it out. Sometimes the Word-washings were like little sponge baths, but this particular morning I felt as though I had been under Niagara Falls.

Attitudes

Our attitudes are indicative of our feelings and moods. They are also indicative of our spiritual maturity. A bad attitude ministers death; whereas a good attitude ministers life. Frank is alert to the significance of my attitudes. Neither am I deaf now when he speaks to me about them.

Respect for Authority

It is a bit awkward when your own husband has to teach you to respect him and all other authority. Happenings do occur, and conflicts between the sexes do arise and often out of them is bred disrespect. The Lord led me to a study of Hannah to show that one should respect the office of one who is in authority, whether the person in the office is a responsible person or not.

Hannah was sorely vexed because she was unable to bear children. She went to the temple to pray and Eli the priest was observing her:

> "So Eli thought she was drunk. Then Eli said to her, 'How long will you make yourself drunk? Put away your wine from you.' But Hannah answered and said, 'No, my lord, I am a woman oppressed in spirit; I have drunk neither wine nor strong drink, but I have poured out my soul before the Lord. Do not consider your maidservant as a worthless woman; for I have spoken until now out of my great concern and provocation' " (I Samuel 1:13b-16).

Here was a woman, greatly distressed, pouring out her heart to the Lord, and her spiritual authority accused her unjustly. This would make the ordinary woman rebel at the unfairness of it all. Notice, though, Hannah called him "my lord"; not because he was a deserving man, but out of respect for the priestly office he filled.

Because she kept her respect for his authority, God blessed her through Eli. Eli said, "Go in peace; and may the God of Israel grant your petition that you have asked of him" (I Samuel 1:17). "So the woman went her way and ate, and her face was no longer sad" (I Samuel 1:18). She kept her attitude right and retained her respect for authority. It all affected her countenance. "Her face was no longer sad."

The story goes on to say that she conceived a short time later. She did not return to the temple until the boy was weaned. Verse twenty-six shows she had not been brooding on the hurt from Eli for again she addresses him as "lord."

"Oh my lord! As your soul lives, my lord, I am the woman who stood here beside you, praying to the Lord. For this boy I prayed, and the Lord has given me my petition which I asked of Him."

Her forgiving attitude kept her from losing respect for her spiritual authority. This put her in a position to receive more children, (five), from the Lord. This was the blessing Hannah sought. It pays to keep respect for authority.

Activities

Daily activities have a way of snowballing. Frank often thought I took on too much. I was a great one to volunteer for everything aside from the things expected of me because I was "the pastor's wife." I really appreciated his stepping in and protecting and disciplining me in this area. It became a challenge to be wiser in self-restraint. We worked at it together, and the result was a big advantage to my nerves. Household harrassment was greatly reduced since I now had more time and strength for my daily chores.

Now, I sometimes get laid back and have to be prodded a bit to get up and get out. So goes the pendulum swings of life. There is never a dull moment.

How to Please My Husband

It is strange that one's own husband would find it necessary to sanctify his wife on how to please him. So many of us are anxious to please everyone except our own husbands. Somehow we can take them for granted and lose the challenge of wanting to please them.

I had to learn to pay attention to the little, low-key suggestions that Frank would make about what pleased him. For example, he wanted our home to be open to hospitality while I did not. I never thought our furniture was nice enough, and it made me nervous to cook for people. When he began to sanctify me, the reasons for my insecurity with entertainment of guests were discovered and overcome.

He had preferences about the kind of clothing I wore, the colors he thought looked best on me, and the style of my hair. But I had my own ideas about what I liked for myself. We wives can be so anxious to please the Lord, and yet the Lord would have us know that one of the ways to please Him is to please our husbands.

How to Love My Husband

It is so easy for the wife to put the children ahead of the husband. If there are several children, it takes time to care for them, and the husband gets shoved back. In my case I had only one daughter, and we had a wonderful relationship. We became companions; and, in many ways, Frank was shut out. Then she grew up and left home. Do you know I wanted to go with her! I was lamenting her leaving and saying I didn't know what I would do, and Frank actually said, "Well, I'm still here." Then I realized I had made a mistake. There had been a shadow in my love for my husband. Do you know that our children can become shadows in our husband-wife relationship?

Sometimes the husband is a strong disciplinarian over the children, and the wife gathers the children around her to protect them from his sternness. Wives, this is wrong. We are to respect our husbands. Husbands need love and respect as much as we wives need love and respect. It is disrespectful to turn our children against their father's authority, and the husband can be wounded by that disrespect. Respect is a form of love.

Another way to love your husband is to pray for him. How are we to pray for husbands? One day the Lord said to me, "Stop praying *Frank's faults.*" Isn't that interesting? I didn't realize that I did that. I was only helping the Lord sanctify him by reminding the lord of the things in him that bugged me. Then the Lord gave me prayers to pray for my husband. I recommend that every wife pray these prayers for her own husband. Some are prayers which Paul prayed for the churches. Look them up and personalize them for your own husband as you pray these prayers for him:

Ephesians 1:16-19
Ephesians 3:14-21
Philippians 1:9-11
Colossians 1:9-14
Hebrews 13:20-21

These are beautiful prayers, and it has helped both of us as I have prayed them. They have helped me to look at my husband in a healthier light, and enabled me to take my sanctifying hands off him, and release him unto God. Then I was able to release myself to my husband for his sanctifying work in me.

Embellishment of Our Good Qualities

We have been talking about a lot of negative qualities in the wives which need sanctification, but I want to say that wives have good qualities of which our husbands also need to lay hold. I have such qualities which my husband seeks to embellish. He will say, "Come on, you can do it. You have a real talent in that. I want to help bring you out so you will have more confidence in yourself."

Concluding Thoughts

What is the purpose in the wife's sanctification? God is strengthening the family, and here is why:

"But the day of the Lord will come like a thief, in which the heavens shall pass away with a roar and the elements will be destroyed with intense heat, and the earth and its works will be burned up. Since all these things are to be destroyed in this way, what sort of people ought you to be in holy conduct and godliness, looking for and hastening the coming of the day of God, on account of which the heavens will be destroyed by burning, and the elements will melt with intense heat! But according to His promise we are looking for new heavens and a new earth, in which righteousness dwells. Therefore, beloved, since you look for these things, BE DILIGENT TO BE FOUND BY HIM IN PEACE, SPOTLESS AND BLAMELESS"* (II Peter 3:10-14).

Wives, will we be found spotless and blameless at His coming? Let those who are given authority over us have that authority. Then, trust God.

One woman who heard me teach this said, "My husband is as lost as a goose, but I can now see that he has been trying to sanctify me. He said I should stop smoking. He has been saying that for some time. I am going to have more respect for what my husband says to me, because God will honor me by speaking through my husband even though he is lost."

At the time of this writing, we have been walking in this principle of sanctification about five years and enjoying its fruits. I am not perfect by any means, but we now have a cohesiveness in our husband/wife relationship that we never had before. I have a stability of purpose that I never had before, and best of all is the unity of body, soul and spirit between us as husband/wife and Jesus our Lord. My individuality has not been taken away, but it has been enhanced by the defining of the boundaries.

Our Bible readings have matured beyond the purpose of my sanctification. Some of Frank's richest revelations from the Word have come during our study time. While I do not have the responsibility of teaching the Word, I do have the blessing and joy of mining the pearls of truth from the Word.

I have been transparent in exposing the things that have happened in my life, because it has brought so much love, and peace and contentment to our home. I pray you, too,

---

*Capitalization for emphasis is mine.

will benefit from our experience. The ways of the Lord are good.

CHAPTER VIII

The Woman's Ministry of Influence

Divine order for the family is not optional. Any family that expects to enjoy the blessings of Kingdom living must function in the kind of family government which God has instituted. Wherever you find a family in which the husband is not fulfilling his scriptural headship and the wife is not in scriptural submission, the devil will be getting his licks. From years of family counseling I have clearly seen that only those families operating in Divine order are not being ravaged by Satan. It is fruitless to try to achieve family unity, peace, love and stability any other way.

Feminist groups today are pushing to make women equal with men in authority and leadership responsibilities. This is unfair to women. It removes them from their place of protection and ladens them with responsibilities for which God did not endow them physically nor emotionally. Christian women have sometimes been deceived by this unscriptural ballyhoo. Satan knows that if he can get the woman out of her role in the family he can have a heyday. So, he tries to make the woman discontented with being a wife and mother; pushes her into the pressures of competition with men, and separates her from her influence over her children.

God does not intend for the woman to be a man. Whenever she tries to be like a man, she must take on an unnatural role and personality; she must become someone other than who she really is. The creation account says "male and female He created them." God created them differently physiologically and temperamentally. He created

111

them for different roles in the family and in life. When a woman decides to take on a man's role, she is rejecting herself. If she wants to be something other than who she is, the devil will help her!

Second, the woman may begin to maneuver in various ways to try to fill a man's role. To compensate for a lack of natural endowment she may manipulate, threaten or use feminine charm to accomplish her goals. Among deliverance ministers this is commonly called "the Jezebel influence." Queen Jezebel employed all of these tactics when she usurped King Ahab's authority, plotted to gain Naboth's vineyard, and determined to intimidate God's prophet. With cunning and deceit she used the King's signet ring of authority to write letters plotting Naboth's death. She threatened Elijah for killing her prophets of Baal. When Jehu came to confront her " . . . she painted her eyes and adorned her head, and looked out the window" (II Kings 9:30). So, Jezebel is typical of women who usurp male authority. But do not overlook the fact that behind every Jezebel is a weak Ahab!

Third, a woman who assumes the male role may take on masculine characteristics. She may begin to walk and gesture like a man, cut her hair in a masculine style, dress in masculine tailored suits and even develop a deep, masculine voice. These traits are demonically acquired. Jezebel is often found in the business world, sometimes in the home and also in the church.

When the woman of the family and church discovers that her place in God is not that of headship or even co-headship, she may think she is unimportant. When the truth of Divine order is taught, it can initially cause some women to feel that they are being robbed of their ministries. They may have been so brainwashed into thinking that ministry is ALWAYS equated with leadership and authority that they cannot envision the greater ministry to which God has called them.

Few women have utilized the powerful ministry God has given them. The woman has a ministry of influence. This is her highest calling. She can use her influence for good or for evil. The world certainly recognizes the woman's influence. Why do you suppose the woman's face and figure are so prominently used in advertising? Even if the advertisement is for a sledge hammer, there will be a picture of a pretty young thing holding it! A woman's picture accompanies almost everything that is sold.

Ladies, you have one of the most powerful weapons ever devised: *Influence*. The first example of woman's influence is found in Eve. After the devil had influenced her, she in turn used her influence to get Adam to eat the forbidden fruit. This is using influence in the wrong way. God will show you in His Word how to channel it for good. Let us examine two positive ways in which the woman can employ her powerful and fruitful ministry of influence.

Influencing Younger Women

"Older women likewise are to be reverent in their behavior, not malicious gossips, not enslaved to much wine, teaching what is good, that they may encourage the young women to love their husbands, to love their children, to be sensible, pure, workers at home, kind, being subject to their own husbands, that the word of God may not be dishonored" (Titus 2:3-5).

The "older women" are not necessarily those older in age, but those older in spiritual maturity. Some women in the church who are advanced in age are not necessarily qualified to teach the younger. Also, "older" is a comparative term. A woman need not be aged to be older than another. Some young women are quite mature in spiritual life and therefore qualified to teach other women who are younger in the Lord.

This ministry of the older women has been one of the most neglected ministries in the church. In too few instances is the maturity of Christian womanhood utilized to mature others. The women can hereby fulfill a ministry that no man can equal, and it is a ministry which is vitally needed. A woman qualifies for this ministry by an example of good behavior. She must be of exemplary character not only before those within the Body of Christ, but also before those who are outside the body.

Six good things are enumerated as examples of important teaching by which the mature women can influence younger women.

1. *To love their husbands and children:* The word for love is "phileo." The Greek expression is one word: husband-lover. The wife and mother is to minister tender affection and warm human love within the family. There are many young women who grew up in families where this kind of love was never demonstrated. How often people tell us that they never saw their parents hug or kiss, and they were never embraced by their parents and told they were loved. Such love is important to offset rejection and insecurity.

A wife may have had a father who was emotionally cold; he may have even abused her. She may have other scars and hurts from men. This can make her uncomfortable and insecure in touching others. Unless these hindrances to love are overcome, she will pass them right on down to her own children, and they will grow up with the same needs that the mother had.

A young wife may never have learned how to express love through thoughtful deeds for her husband. She needs to be taught to keep his shirts washed and pressed, or to prepare his favorite dish, or to meet him at the door with a big hug and words of appreciation when he comes in from work.

It is tragic when family members take one another for granted. Each family needs heavy doses of love. The husband is told to love his wife with "agape" love. This is the sacrificial love that Christ had for the church. The wife is told to love her family with "phileo" love. This kind of love is expressed through touch, words and deeds.

2. *To be sensible:* The King James translation says

"discrete." (See Titus 2:5.) This means to be self-controlled, having the passions curbed.

3. *To be pure:* This means to be modest and free of evil and defilement.

4. *To be workers at home:* That is, to be good housekeepers and homemakers: to be proficient in domestic duties such as cooking, sewing and cleaning. I have been surprised to find many women who never learned how to keep a house clean and in order. Outward filth and clutter is indicative of an inward problem. I have yet to find a spiritually disciplined person who was not also disciplined in the natural life. In our own fellowship the older women have taught the younger ones how to can vegetables, prepare food for the freezer, dehydrate food, make bread, and many other things.

A woman needs to understand that housekeeping is a ministry with eternal rewards when it is performed "as to the Lord." A few years ago I was talking to a well-known minister and his wife. The wife was discouraged because she felt that she had no valid ministry. Her husband interviewed others on Christian television every day. She would listen to those interviews of people doing all sorts of things while she just stayed at home and kept house and looked after the children. Ida Mae and I had the opportunity to share with her the importance of what she was doing and how it was a valid ministry. It was her calling. It was a blessed revelation to her, and she became content in "just being" a good wife and mother.

5. *To be kind:* The King James translation says "good." (See Titus 2:5.) This word means to be good-natured, pleasant, agreeable, joyful and happy. Who wants to come home to an old grouch? The wife has much influence in setting the atmosphere in the home.

6. *To be subject to their own husbands:* This is the same word for submission that we have already discussed. Remember it

means to be set in array, to be set in the position of Divine order. The root word means "to pay attention; to listen." A wife needs to be a good listener. The husband often speaks through little hints rather than saying something outright. A listening wife will hear all the little hints and suggestions because her desire is to please her husband and do those things which bless him.

What a ministry of teaching! It is not a formal ministry where one stands behind a pulpit or lectern and delivers a studied-out message. It is one-on-one or small group ministry among the women of the church. It is informal, practical and personal. It reaches into the lives of the younger women, changing them into Christlikeness. Its influence permeates the whole family where this teaching is deposited. The older woman's influence of good teaching flows through the younger women to the husbands and children. A whole generation is influenced for God, and that influence passes down to succeeding generations. There are going to be some surprises when the Lord passes out the rewards. Some women who were never in the public eye will receive some of the biggest crowns.

Influencing Husbands

"In the same way, you wives, be submissive to your own husbands so that even if any of them are disobedient to the word, they may be won without a word by the behavior of their wives, as they observe your chaste and respectful behavior. And let not your adornment be merely external – braiding the hair, and wearing gold jewelry, or putting on dresses; but let it be the hidden person of the heart, with the imperishable quality of a gentle and quiet spirit, which is precious in the sight of God. For in this way in former times the holy women also, who hoped in God, used to adorn themselves, being submissive to their own husbands. Thus Sarah obeyed Abraham, calling him lord, and you have become her children if you do what is right without being frightened by any fear" (I Peter 3:1-6).

This is a most important passage for any wife who is burdened over the spiritual condition of her husband. In the circles where I have pastored and ministered I have found more dedicated Christian women than men. Many women are seeking prayer for lost, backslidden and indifferent husbands. This Scripture fits all these categories of husbands, for it is applicable to any who are "disobedient to the word." Here is a God-given formula for the wife desiring spiritual improvement in her husband. Remember, however, that God's counsel must be followed exactly. There is no place for substitution of one's own way. There are four distinct avenues of influence that a wife can use:

1. *Submission:* "In the same way, you wives, be submissive to your own husbands." In the same way as what? This phrase requires us to to back in the context to chapter two, verse eighteen. There it is talking about the submission of a servant to his master. Peter, the inspired writer of Scripture, is saying that a wife is to submit to her husband in the same way that a servant is required to submit to his master. Thus:

> "Servants, be submissive to your masters with all respect, not only to those who are good and gentle, but also to those who are unreasonable" (I Peter 2:18).

Submission is a position of influence. The opposite of submission is independence, self-will and rebellion from which stance a wife's influence is nil. It is admittedly much easier for a wife to submit to a husband who is always kind, sweet, patient, understanding, thoughtful and helpful, but God's Word calls for submission to husbands who are "unreasonable." The Amplified Bible adds "surly – overbearing, unjust and crooked." One must admit that describes many husbands who are not following the Lord. Such men need all the spiritual influence a wife can muster in the Lord.

A husband who is not guided and motivated by Divine love will cause the wife much unjust suffering. Verse nineteen tells us that a servant or wife who bears up under unjust suffering for the sake of conscience toward God finds favor with God. If one has favor with God, it means that God will work in behalf of that person and reward him accordingly.

A wife with a hard-to-live-with husband must decide between standing up for her rights or submitting for the sake of winning her husband to the Lord through her godly influence. One thing is certain: without submission a wife has lost her power of influence and thereby departed from God's counsel on how to turn him around spiritually.

God's Word says husbands may be won without a word by the behavior of their wives. The influence of submission is stronger than words. A wife must seek God's strength daily to guard her mouth against criticism, needling or browbeating to bring the husband around. Such tactics only deepen his stubborness.

2. *Chaste behavior:* This phrase signifies purity, holiness and freedom from every fault. A lost and backslidden husband will watch his Christian wife closely for any flaw in character, and he will usually throw it up to her if he catches her in a fault. A lapse in godly behavior gives him an excuse to justify his own shortcomings and to blaspheme the name of Christ.

It is most common that an ungodly husband will purposely put pressure on his wife to cause her to react in anger, crying or the like. This is done to make himself look as good as he can and to discredit her Christian testimony. There are several instances in my memory where wives were doing their best to live faultlessly before their husbands, but in times of pressure created by their husbands, they reacted sinfully. Their influence was shipwrecked. What could they do then? They had to start over. Before the wife's influence can be effective it must be exemplary.

3. *Respectful behavior:* Other translations say "fear" or "reverence." This Greek word "phobos" is used to describe our reverential fear of God, a wholesome dread of displeas-

ing Him. The Amplified Bible, in I Peter 3:2, uses the word "reverence" and amplifies the meaning thusly: "to respect, defer to, revere him: [revere means] to honor, esteem (appreciate, prize), and [in a human sense] adore him; [and adore means] to admire, praise, be devoted to, deeply love and enjoy [your husband]."

If a wife has lost respect for her husband, she must work to regain it. If she is to maintain her influence, she must uphold him in every way. This means she will not permit herself to criticize him publicly or privately. She will not even share her husband's faults with her best friend. To regain lost respect she must begin to verbally and outwardly express her appreciation for her husband. She must compliment everything that she can find worthy about him.

There is nothing a husband needs and desires from his wife more than respect. A wife needs to be loved and a husband needs to be respected. Since a man desires respect so very much, if he gets a little from his wife he will probably work hard to get more. Few men ever change because their wives call all their faults to their attention. Any meaningful change in the husband must come from within his heart and be self-motivated. This is the purpose of the wife's influence. When a man is respected, he is encouraged to try harder to deserve respect.

4. *Inward adorning:* Any woman knows that she can get a man's attention by having a nice coiffure and wearing a pretty dress with accessories. But to what in a man does such adornment appeal? His flesh! A man will not be influenced spiritually through sex appeal. This passage is not a proof-text for not wearing makeup and pretty hairdos. It is saying that a man is not influenced spiritually by these means. In order to draw him closer to the Lord, a wife must adorn the inner person of the heart with a "gentle and quiet spirit." This means that she will be poised under pressure. Such adorning is "precious in the sight of God."

Should the husband become angry and rail at the wife,

she, who is adorned with a gentle and quiet spirit, will remain calm under the attack. If in the past she has succumbed to hysteria or responded with anger, that husband will begin to wonder what caused the difference. Sooner or later he will have to recognize that it is the Spirit of God in her that has made the difference.

How is a woman ever able to come to such a condition of poise? The context goes on to tell us how. She will do it in the same way as holy women have done it in time past: by their hope in God.

The woman's ability to remain poised under pressure is through hope in God. If a woman does not stand in hope, she will react in the flesh. Hope is "an anchor of the soul" (Hebrews 6:19): an anchor to the mind, emotions and will.

Sarah is singled out as an example to follow in submission, good behavior, respect and inner adornment. She obeyed Abraham, calling him "lord." When we recall the two times in Old Testament history when Abraham required Sarah to conceal her identity as his wife and say that she was only his sister (she was actually his half sister) and all the pressures these circumstances put Sarah under, we can appreciate the hope she maintained in God which enabled her to submit to Abraham and still retain her respect for him.

Sarah called Abraham "lord" (Genesis 18:12). This was a title of respect. We had a good laugh when Ida Mae and I were studying all this out for the sake of her own submission. She raised this question: "Isn't it true that in the original manuscripts there was no punctuation, and that punctuation was added when the Bible was translated?" I assured her this was true. She said, "I think they mispunctuated it here. When Abraham asked Sarah to protect his life by saying she was his sister she didn't say, 'My lord, Abraham;' she said, 'My Lord! Abraham!' "

The context of I Peter, chapter three, goes right on to apply to the principle of the wife's influence through her godly behavior. Reflect carefully on these verses as they apply to the wife's poise under pressure.

"To sum up, let all be harmonious, sympathetic, brother-
ly, kindhearted, and humble in spirit; not returning evil
for evil, or insult for insult, but giving a blessing instead;
for you were called for the very purpose that you might
inherit a blessing, For,
    'Let him who means to love life and see good days
    Refrain his tongue from evil and from speaking guile.
    And let him turn away from evil and do good;
    Let him seek peace and pursue it.
    For the eyes of the Lord are upon the righteous,
    And His ears attend to their prayer,
    But the face of the Lord is against those who do evil.'

"And who is there to harm you if you prove zealous for
what is good? But even if you should suffer for the sake
of righteousness, you are blessed. And do not fear their
intimidation, and do not be troubled, but sanctify Christ
as Lord in your hearts, always being ready to make a
defense to everyone who asks you to give an account for
the hope that is in you, yet with gentleness and reverence;
and keep a good conscience so that in the thing in which
you are slandered, those who revile your good behavior
in Christ may be put to shame. For it is better, if God
should will it so, that you suffer for doing what is right
rather than for doing what is wrong" (I Peter 3:8-17).

A Christian wife is in the best position of anyone to influence a husband for the Lord. She lives with him and the
two are "one flesh." From a position of hope and trust in
God she must consistently, thoroughly and patiently channel her influence as God has counseled. Here it is again:

1. Submit yourselves to your own husbands as unto the
Lord in everything.

2. Keep your behavior completely Christlike.

3. Respect your husband as the God-appointed head of
the family.

4. Adorn your inner person with the imperishable quality of a gentle and quiet spirit.

CHAPTER IX

Bringing Up Children in the Lord

It is a real challenge to bring up children in the Lord, to bring them into the full blessings of Kingdom living and under the Lordship of Jesus Christ. There are many spiritual battles which must be fought. Parents themselves must be close to the Lord and walking in His ways. They must be consistent in their own spiritual lives and diligent in the application of spiritual principles toward the children.

The command to bring up children in the Lord is given to the parents. The direct responsibility is given to the father:

> "And, fathers, do not provoke your children to anger; but bring them up in the discipline and instruction of the Lord" (Ephesians 6:4).

The church and its Sunday school may assist the parents in their God-given responsibility, but God never intended for the church, the Sunday school teacher, the Christian school nor any other agency or person to assume the burden of bringing up children in the ways of God.

In Israel there were thousands of priests who were trained in the Word of God and in ministering unto the Lord. But the priests were not given charge to bring up the children of the people in the ways of God. This charge was given by God to parents.

Because the church has set up a program for the religious education and spiritual training of children, parents have often assumed that it is the church's responsibility rather than their own. Parents send their children to Sunday school as a substitute for their own responsibility, and the children receive little or no training at home.

The spiritual upbringing of children is a full-time and daily matter. There is no way that a child can receive all his necessary teaching and training through an hour or two in a classroom situation, and nowhere in the New Testament is the church given that task.

Teaching Children

The Bible sets the pattern for teaching and training children in the ways of God. It calls for day-in and day-out diligence on the part of the parents.

> "And you shall love the Lord your God with all your heart and with all your soul and with all your might. And these words, which I am commanding you today, shall be on your heart; and you shall teach them diligently to your sons and shall talk of them when you sit in your house and when you walk by the way and when you lie down and when you rise up. And you shall bind them as a sign on your hand and they shall be as frontals on your forehead. And you shall write them on the doorposts of your house and on your gates" (Deuteronomy 6:5-9).

Several guiding principles are set forth in this passage. First, parents must become qualified to lead their children into the life of God. Parents cannot lead except through the example of their own lives. If children are to grow up with Christ as their priority, they must see the consistent example of parents loving the Lord with their whole heart, soul and might. If children are to grow up respecting the Word of God as "a lamp unto their feet and a light unto their path," they must be molded into that pattern of conviction by parents who display in their own lives an unfailing obedience to God's Word.

Children are the responsibility of the parents who gave them birth. And parents must "teach them diligently." The Hebrew people used very expressive words. Their word for

123

"teach" means to sharpen: to whet. Teaching a child was compared to whetting a knife. A knife is sharpened by a diligent process of over-and-over, back-and-forth on a whetstone. A child's understanding is sharpened by going over and over the things to be learned. This requires much patience.

Parents usually have many things on their minds. Mothers get involved with housework, shopping, calls, entertainment, and many other things. Fathers are busy at the office or shop, watching television in the evenings, playing golf, keeping the yard mowed, and other things. So, if children are to get the "whetting" they need to develop into spiritually mature persons, they must be made a priority.

When this Scripture says that children must be taught the Word of God from the moment of awakening each day until they are put to bed at night, it is not talking about classroom type instruction. It does not mean that you set the children before you and give them a textbook lesson. Instead, it means that children need to be taught the principles of Bible truth through daily events and circumstances.

For example, if a child becomes interested in a little bird that has fallen out of its nest, the parents have a tailor-made opportunity to teach the child about God's creation, man's stewardship over creation, and God's care for us, because He notices the fall of every sparrow.

If a child gets into conflict with a playmate over who gets to ride the bicycle first, it is an opportunity to teach a good lesson on unselfishness, preferring others, returning good for evil, forgiveness and much more.

The thrust of what God is saying is that parents must keep the Word of God so thoroughly before the lives of their children that obedience to God's Word will become the disciplined pattern of thought and behavior. They will learn to act in obedience without giving it further thought. In their minds and hearts there will be no alternative to following God's truth.

124

The ancient Jews wore phylacteries on their hands and foreheads. These were small boxes containing a parchment upon which was written Deuteronomy 6:4-9 and other basic commandments. These were reminders to keep God's law in mind and practice. Phylacteries have a spiritual application. Parents must first have God's Word in their own minds continually and must be faithful doers of God's Word in order to bring up children in the Word.

> "When your son asks you in time to come saying, 'What do the testimonies and the statutes and the judgments mean which the Lord commanded you?' Then you shall say to your son, 'We were slaves to Pharaoh in Egypt; and the Lord brought us from Egypt with a mighty hand. Moreover, the Lord showed great and distressing signs and wonders before our eyes against Egypt, Pharaoh and all his household; and He brought us out from there in order to bring us in, to give us the land which He had sworn to our fathers. So the Lord commanded us to observe all these statutes, to fear the Lord our God for our good always and for our survival, as it is today. And it will be righteousness for us if we are careful to observe all this commandment before the Lord our God, just as He commanded us' " (Deuteronomy 6:20-25).

As children grow up they are to learn the whole truth of God. The "testimonies, statutes and judgments" represent the complete revelation of God. The religious ceremonies would evoke questions from the children. As they grow older they will ask, "Why do we do these things?" Older children need explanations. Parents must have answers.

Can the average Christian parent answer his son's or daughter's questions about water baptism or the Lord's supper? Here are opportunities to teach the basic truths of the Gospel.

There are many important truths in the Old Testament histories. Paul said this concerning Israel's experiences in being delivered from Egyptian bondage and living in the wilderness:

"Now these things happened to them as an example, and they are written for our instruction, upon whom the ends of the ages have come" (I Corinthians 10:11).

Fathers are commanded to bring up their children in the "admonition of the Lord" (Ephesians 6:4, Kings James version). The word "admonition" literally means to put into mind. We ask, "Put what into their minds?" The Word of God! Let us examine two passages of Scripture which illustrate two facets of admonition:

In I Corinthians 10:11, (See quotation above) what happened to Israel is said to be "for our admonition." These accounts put into our minds how God deals with His people. Admonition provides information and motivation. We see what happened to the Israelites because of their sins. God punished them. So we must get it into our minds not to do the things which they did if we expect to avoid God's judgment.

In Titus 3:10, King James version, we are told to reject a heretic "after the first and second admonition." Here, admonition means to give warning; to reprove or to correct. Troublemakers in the church are admonished with a view to bringing them back in line with God. Children are to be admonished in the same sense. If a child is caught lying, he should be admonished by the Scriptures. "Thou shall not bear false witness" would be an excellent example.

Bible memorization is another way of putting God's Word into the minds of children. Parents must teach their children to memorize key Scriptures. These memorized passages will be woven into their hearts, and when they grow up they will say with the Psalmist. "Thy word I have treasured in my heart, that I may not sin against Thee" (Psalm 119:11).

Training Children

"Train up a child in the way he should go, Even when he is old he will not depart from it" (Proverbs 22:6).

126

Some parents have misunderstood this verse. When a child has gone into rebellion and worldiness, some have said, "But I sent him to Sunday school, I told him he shouldn't run with the wrong crowd, and I gave him everything his little heart desired. I just don't understand why he has gone astray." The command to "train up a child in the way he should go" is a positive admonition to keep a child diligently in the narrow way of God's instructions.

There is a difference between teaching and training. The Hebrew word for "train" means "to make narrow." Jesus taught that the way of life is straight and narrow. He taught His disciples to walk in a narrow path: the path of obedience to God.

This kind of training is the opposite of some modern-day philosophies that advocate permissiveness and letting the child do what comes naturally. God's narrow way is the road to peace and safety. His way leads to victorious life here on earth and to eternal life. Children must be trained to walk in the narrow ways of God where the roaring lion cannot catch and devour them.

> "My son, observe the commandment of your father,
> And do not forsake the teaching of your mother;
> Bind them continually on your heart;
> Tie them around your neck.
> When you walk about, they will guide you;
> When you sleep, they will watch over you;
> When you awake, they will talk to you.
> For the commandment is a lamp, and the teaching is light;
> And reproofs for discipline are the way of life"
> (Proverbs 6:20-23).

In Ephesians 6:4, Amplified version, fathers are commissioned to bring up their children "in the nurture . . . of the Lord." This word "nuture" primarily denotes "to train."

A pastor friend of mine had a large collie which he obtained for his children. This dog was by nature a very gentle animal. In order to keep it from jumping up on people and becoming a nuisance rather than a pleasure, he realized it must be trained. So, he spent an hour each day for several weeks training the collie to obey. He loved this dog, but he required it to obey. Within a short time the dog became a well-trained and obedient pet. It was a pleasure to be with this dog. In like manner children can and must be trained. If the parent loves the child, he will train the child; obedience will be consistently required. When properly trained, a child will become self-disciplined and a rest to the parents.

"The rod and reproof give wisdom, But a child who gets his own way brings shame to his mother" (Proverbs 29:15).

Training children must be done in love with firmness. Firmness is applied in two ways: First, by correction with words of reproof and, second, with chastening blows, also called scourging. The example of chastening has been set by the Heavenly Father.

"And you have forgotten the exhortation which is addressed to you as sons, 'My son, do not regard lightly the discipline of the Lord, nor faint when you are reproved by Him; For those whom the Lord loves He disciplines, and He scourges every son whom He receives.' It is for dicipline that you endure; God deals with you as with sons, for what son is there whom his father does not discipline? But if you are without discipline, of which all have become partakers, then you are illegitimate children and not sons. Furthermore, we had earthly fathers to discipline us, and we respected them; shall we not much rather be subject to the Father of spirits, and live? For they disciplined us for a short time as seemed best to them, but He disciplines us for our good, that we may share His holiness. All discipline for the moment seems not to be joyful, but sorrowful; yet to those who have trained by it, afterwards it yields the peaceful fruit of righteousness" (Hebrews 12:5-11).

Children are also trained by example. They quickly learn to do whatever the parents do – whether good or bad. It is unrealistic for a parent to expect something better or something different than the example set before the child. It is the same as with a pastor's example before his people. Paul exhorted the young pastor Timothy:

> "... in speech, conduct, love, faith and purity, show yourself an example" (I Timothy 4:12).

Whatever influence is established in a family will pass down from generation to generation. This is why it is so imperative for parents to set the right example.

King Ahaziah was a very wicked king, but he was only following the example of his parents, Ahab and Jezebel. The biblical record gives this account:

> "Ahaziah the son of Ahab became King over Israel in Samaria in the seventeenth year of Jehoshaphat king of Judah, and he reigned two years over Israel. And he did evil in the sight of the Lord and walked in the way of his father and in the way of his mother and in the way of Jeroboam the son of Nebat, who caused Israel to sin. So he served Baal and worshipped him and provoked the Lord God of Israel to anger according to all that his father had done" (I Kings 22:51-53).

Then the next generation, the grandson of Ahab, produced another wicked Ahaziah whose mother was the wicked Athaliah.

> "He also walked in the ways of the house of Ahab, for his mother was his counselor to do wickedly. And he did evil in the sight of the Lord like the house of Ahab, for they were his counselors after the death of his father, to his destruction" (II Chronicles 22:3-4).

Thus, we see the evil influence passing down through a family. Nevertheless, there is one thing that will reverse such an evil trend: the grace of God. One who is the product of wrong influence can become "the righteousness of God in Christ." In Christ he becomes a new creation: old things pass away and all things become new. This seed of new life is planted in a person at the time of new birth. The potential of change is present with every regenerated person.

> "Therefore consider the members of your earthly body as dead to immorality, impurity, passion, evil desire, and

greed, which amounts to idolatry . . . and have put on the new self who is being renewed to a true knowledge according to the image of the One who created him" (Colosians 3:5,10).

Another important aspects of training children in the Lord is through the application of God's Word to life situations. Suppose a son comes home from school and is upset because someone stole his new notebook, or another boy picked a fight with him, or the teacher punished him unjustly. The wise parent will take full advantage of such everyday events to train his son to apply God's teachings to life situations. Unless such training is provided, this son can become bitter, resentful and rebellious; or, on the other hand, become filled with self-pity, insecurity and rejection. He may become belligerent or else withdraw into himself.

Family participation in Bible study, prayer and worship is important to nuturing children in the Lord. I thank God for the years of family altar, which was a part of my daily life from birth onward. My brothers and I were required to be at the breakfast table on time. After breakfast together the family remained at the table until we had finished a season of family worship as father read a portion of Scripture and led us in prayer. Even the training I received through church services and Sunday school was not to be compared to the valuable training I received at the feet of my earthly father.

As parents bring up children in the Lord, let them realize the far-reaching results of their efforts. Their children are being molded into stable, Christian people who will serve God all the days of their lives and pass a rich spiritual heritage on down to their children and their children's children. Futhermore, the solid spiritual foundation provided them will enable them to weather the storms of life. (See Matthew 7:24-27.)

Children are the products of the family. They are exactly what the parents bring them up to be. As little children they are tender plants; their lives are impressionable and easily directed. The process of training a child can be compared to training a grapevine to grow on a trellis. The tender tendrils are directed by the hands of the vinedresser. A branch that has fallen down is lifted up and given new direction. This grape-vine analogy impresses us that the time to train children is early in life. By the time they are a few years old, many of their life's patterns are already set.

No two children are alike in personality. Each child is an individual and must be treated as such by the parents. Training, in many ways, must be personalized according to the individual needs of the child. The objective is not to have each child fit a certain mold, but to direct him to be an individual person who will serve and glorify God in his own way.

A family may have several children, and each of them be different in talents, interests and abilities. However, each must be molded in Christlikeness of character. The molding of character is the direct result of teaching, training, discipline and love. The wise parent will direct the child's special talents, interests and abilities into desirable channels and mold his behavior patterns to conform to the standards of God's Word.

If a mother says, "I just don't know what makes little Billy act like that; he just embarrasses me so," she is reflecting her failure to understand and practice proper child discipline and confessing her failure to be consistent, diligent and firm in training her child.

It would indeed be a surprise if little Billy needed no correction. He was born with an Adamic nature prone to sin. It is the parent's business to curb these evil tendencies in the life of the child.

> "Foolishness is bound up in the heart of a child; The rod
> of discipline will remove it far from him" Proverbs 22:15).

An old adage is correct which says, "As the twig is bent, so shall it grow." Both a twig and a child can be directed in the way it should grow.

God does not require the impossible. When He says, "Fathers, bring up your children . . . in the Lord," He is commanding something that every father is able to do. The reason it is possible is that the father has every Divine resource needed in order to accomplish that goal. No father is left to his own wisdom; he has the Word of God and the guidance of the Holy Spirit. When he is guided by these infallible sources, he cannot fail. His children will grow up to be an honor to him and a blessing. As he brings them up in the way they should go, he can be at peace in knowing that they will not depart from their training. That is God's promise.

Bringing up children "in the Lord" means foremost to bring them up to know the Lord personally. No child is saved because his parents are born again. Each child must individually repent of his sins and confess Christ as Savior.

The boy Samuel was dedicated to the Lord by his parents, and as soon as he was weaned he was placed under the care of Eli, the priest. He grew up in the tabernacle, acquainted with the sacrifices and ministries unto God. However, it is said that he did not yet know the Lord. Then, there came a day in Samuel's life when God called him personally by name. When Eli realized that it was the Lord speaking directly to young Samuel, he had the wisdom to teach Samuel how to respond to God's call.

In a similar fashion, a father as priest in his home will bring up his children in a spiritual atmosphere. From the time of birth, each child will be exposed to the truths of God. The worship of God in the home and church will be a natural part of the child's daily experience. He will observe the family's respect for prayer and the Bible. He will become familiar with the Scriptures and will learn of the great sacrifice that Jesus Christ made on the cross. Then, one day, the Lord will call him by name, just as he did Samuel. The father/priest will recognize this call and will lead his child to answer God's call to salvation.

This is exactly the way it happened in my own life. I was brought up in the ways of God. The Word of God, worship and prayer were a part of my daily life. I learned how Jesus became a man, lived a sinless life and died on the cross as my substitute. yet at the age of nine I had not made the application of Christ's death to my own life. Finally, the Lord began to speak to my young heart. A few days before my tenth birthday, my father recognized God's dealing in my life. He had me sit down with him in the living room of our home and there taught me how to answer God's call. I confessed my sins, called upon Jesus to save me and was born again.

Again, this is exactly how it happened with our daughter. She was brought up from birth in a spiritual atmosphere at home and at church. When she was six years of age, we were in a church service one Wednesday night when she began to weep. Her mother was sitting next to her and asked her what was the matter. She replied, "The preacher said, 'Joyce, you are a sinner.' " Of course the pastor had not said these words, but in her heart she was hearing God's call to repentance and salvation. Her mother whispered to me what was happening and we directed our daughter to answer God's call. She went forward in that service and acknowledged publicly that she was accepting the Lord Jesus Christ as her personal Savior.

Christ commissioned His church to evangelize the whole world. This work of evangelism may take place on the mission field, in a church evangelistic campaign or on the streets of the city. However, the evangelization of children in the home is the privilege and responsibility of the parents. Although we thank God for pastors and church workers who lead children to Christ when the parents are unqualified because of their own lost and backslidden condition; or, when the parents neglect this eternally important responsibility, yet it is best for parents to lead their own children into salvation. Parents who are walking with the Lord know when the Lord is beginning to speak to their child. There is no certain age when this takes place. The parents who have faithfully kept the truths of God's Word and the right spiritual examples before the child, will anticipate the call of God to salvation and be alert to guide the child in his new-birth experience.

Since salvation requires a heart response, as opposed to a mere head response, a child must not be prematurely coerced into a decision. The membership rolls of some churches have become choked with the names of children who were manipulated into "making a decision for Christ" and were not genuinely born from above. This is why it is the ideal for parents who know their child and are sensitive to the Holy Spirit's moving to guide their child into personal salvation at the earliest possible time and not force the child into a premature and false commitment. A father bringing up a child in the Lord includes the important step of bringing him to the Lord in personal salvation.

Also, bringing up children in the Lord involves bringing them up in God's counsel. It seems that everyone today poses as a counselor. There are many would-be counselors standing by to counsel our children. The world has its ranks of counselors operating through government agencies, public schools, boys' and girls' organizations, special children's programs in the community, relatives, neighbors, religious zealots on the street corners and others. Few of these can be depended upon to give your children God's unadulterated counsel. In fact, they have not been authorized by God to give such counsel to YOUR children! All counsel given to children should be screened and approved by the "fathers" whom God has commissioned to bring up children in the Lord.

Jesus is called "Wonderful Counselor." His counsel is all that is needed. His counsel for bringing up children in the Lord is complete counsel. If a parent attempts to supplement God's counsel with worldly counsel, he will only introduce a damaging mixture. Sound counsel is found only in the words of our all-wise God. Any counsel that does not line up with His Word is worthless and harmful. The world cannot give sound counsel, for Satan is the "god of this world." The believer is warned against following worldly counsel: "Walk not in the counsel of the ungodly." The world's counsel will always be ungodly counsel. The reason for this is apparent.

> "But the natural man does not accept the things of the Spirit of God; for they are foolishness to him, and he cannot understand them, because they are spiritually appraised" (I Corinthians 2:14).

Disciplining Children

In the minds of many the word discipline means punishment. Discipline may involve punishment, but its principle meaning is "to teach." The purpose of punishment as discipline is to teach a child obedience, to choose right rather than wrong, and to govern his own actions.

The word "discipline" is a form of the word "disciple." Thus, the parent is a disciplinarian, the child is a disciple and the process of teaching and training the child is discipleship.

A disciple is a learner, a pupil. Through proper discipline a child arrives at the goal of self-control and self-discipline. The punishment aspect of discipline is usually unpleasant for both parent and child, but must never be avoided nor postponed for that reason. Indeed, parents are not expected to enjoy spanking their children anymore than the child is expected to enjoy the spanking. It is, therefore, done out of the necessity to produce a disciplined child in spite of its being an unpleasant factor in parent-child relationship.

The Heavenly Father does not enjoy punishing His children, but it is necessary, and He does it. This is the position a good parent must take. To do so, the parent must keep his eye on the goal to be achieved. A disciplined child will be a blessing to the family, to himself, and others. God calls the result "the peaceable fruit of righteousness" (Hebrews

12:11). The child is brought to right relationship with God, his family and society. Everyone is at peace with him because he is a peaceful child.

On the other hand, the undisciplined or improperly disciplined child becomes a brat. Any child can readily "go wild" if not properly managed. He will become a burden and even a menace. A parent should be motivated to discipline his child if for no other reason than the peace it will bring to oneself.

> "The rod and reproof give wisdom, but a child who gets his own way brings shame to his mother" (Proverbs 15:15).

Children are not capable of raising themselves. They cannot be expected to arrive at self-discipline and righteous character apart from thorough and consistent discipline. Parents often need help in becoming good disciplinarians. This kind of instruction should come from the pulpits and classrooms of our churches. The church should be concerned with preaching sound doctrine, and Paul exhorts young Titus to preach sound doctrine by giving practical instruction on behavior, character and relationships with each person in the family. (See Titus 2:1-15.)

Some parents do not provide proper discipline for their children simply because they are undisciplined themselves. They were not properly disciplined by their own parents and have no pattern to follow. The concerned parent will want to learn to be a good parent and will find help through his church or through Christian literature. The world's wisdom cannot be trusted to give sound instruction. Parents who honestly do not know how to love and train their children may be criticized and judged by others who say, "Why don't they do something with that child?" Such parents may never have been awakened to the need or instructed in the "hows" of child discipline. The undisciplined parent will not be helped by fault-finders, but by competent counselors.

The church has a special interest in teaching the family because the church is made up of families. Just as a house is no stronger than the materials that go into it, so the church is no stronger than its families. A church full of stable, happy families will be a stable, happy church. What pastor does not want an orderly, disciplined church body? How can there be a disciplined church without a disciplined people?

Now, let us move on to talk about scriptural discipline for children. First, we find that God places the responsibility for child discipline upon the father. God commands:

And, fathers . . . bring them up in the discipline and instruction of the Lord" (Ephesians 6:4).

Thus, it is clear that God has made the father accountable for the discipline of the children. This is one of his major responsibilities as head of the family. This is not to say that the father does it all himself, but that he takes the lead and gives oversight to all that is done. It is an unfair burden to a mother to have to administer all the punishment to her children. She, of necessity, must assume some of the responsibility and cooperate with the father's leadership.

It is of utmost importance that mother and father be in agreement in matters of child discipline. For example, if the mother feels the father is too hard on the children, she can easily become resentful of him and feel that she must protect her children from their father. This, in turn, ministers confusion to the children, and they begin to play one parent against the other by taking advantage of the more lenient one and siding with mother in her resentment. Whatever it takes to get two parents into unity over discipline should be done, because the children will suffer the consequences until unity is achived.

The differences between mother and father may not mean that one is wrong and the other right. Usually, some adjustments are needed on both sides. For example, the father may be too harsh. It is possible for him to punish the children out of frustration, impatience, and anger. He may slap them around, because that is the way his father treated him. Then, again, the mother may be too soft and fearful that the children will be scared. But, whatever the reason for the differences, the solution should be pursued diligently through Bible study, prayer, open communication, pastoral counseling and deliverance.

One common mistake is to give punishment authority over younger children to an older brother or sister. This creates problems for all concerned. Any child lacks the mature wisdom needed for such an important responsibility. It is unfair to require it of him. The younger child will become confused over authority, and usually develop a strong resentment toward the older brother or sister. The older child is prone to become bossy and, at the same time, resentful toward his parents. All of the children involved may develop wrong ideas and attitudes about punishment that will carry into adulthood and adversely affect their ability to correct their own children later on. Parents who are overbearing or else too lenient usually become that way due to wrong discipline practices in their own lives.

What is to be done about punishment when children are left in care of others: grandparents, baby sitters, child care facilities, or others? First, we must not forget the basic principle that the father is responsible for his children. He and the mother should be very careful about who cares for them and what kind of treatment they receive.

Sometimes the parents will need to give punishment authority to another. This depends on the length of time involved. If the child is in another's care for only a few hours, then punishment authority is rarely needed. Any need for punishment can be reported to the parent who will administer it at his discretion. In other instances, when another cares for the child for extended periods of time, delegated punishment privileges become more important. To be the most effective, the punishment should be in close time proximity to the offense. It cannot wait until another authority arrives, or else a small child may not even know why he is being punished.

A definite understanding should exist when delegated authority is granted. The parent has both the right and responsibility to set the terms and extent of punishment allowable. The parent should make it a point to know what is happening.

Now let us go on to talk about what is scriptural punishment for children. There is a negative and positive side to this matter. The Scripture gives warning as well as counsel:

> "And, fathers, do not provoke your children to anger" (Ephesians 6:4).

> "Fathers, do not exasperate your children, that they may not lose heart" (Colossians 3:21).

> " . . . lest they become discouraged and sullen and morose and feel inferior and frustrated; do not break their spirit" (Colossians 3:21, Amplified Bible).

This is a warning not to abuse a child through physical abuse or unreasonable punishment and treatment. Such treatment may wound or cripple a child physically, but the emphasis in the Scripture is upon the wounding of personality. Genuine wisdom is required. A rebellious child is sometimes defiant in his will. The stubborn will must be broken, but not the child's spirit. The goal is to produce pliableness without creating anger, resentment, discouragement, inferiority, self-pity or frustration in the process.

Harm to a child's personality can result not only from the wrong degree of punishment, but, also from the wrong *kind* of punishment. Prolonged forms of punishment create an atmosphere that can breed bad attitudes and emotions. These may be vented in open hostility or buried deep inside only to erupt later in life, when he thinks he is old enough to get away with it.

The Scripture is completely silent on punishment techniques that are commonly accepted and practiced today. The Word of God does not counsel parents to withhold privileges. There is no ground for sending one's child to bed without

139

his supper, pinching, pulling his hair, slapping the face or requiring him to stand in the corner.

A parent must avoid being more concerned with venting his own anger, frustration or revenge than in correcting the child. The child relates to such punishment as abuse and resentment toward his parent takes root. There is only one method of punishment counseled by Scripture, and the parent will not go wrong in adopting the *rod* as the only necessary form of punishment. What is meant by a rod and what governs its use? The rod is not a magic wand that brings the desired results just because it is a rod. The exact features of the rod used for punishment are not nearly as important as the factors involved in its employment.

The common Hebrew word for "rod" is "shebet." It is simply a stick, a staff or a rod used for chastening. Common sense will tell you that the size of the rod should be in keeping with the size of the child. All that is needed is to induce just enough pain to the buttocks to bring about the desired correction.

Because of the increased incidents of battered and abused children, some are advocating the total banning of the rod as a valid instrument of punishment. In Sweden, for example, it is unlawful for parents to spank their children. While ministering in Sweden we questioned pastors and parents as to whether this law is enforced. We were told that a parent could receive six months in jail for spanking his child and a year in jail if the spanking left marks on the child. We observed that some Christian parents had very unruly and undisciplined children, because they were intimidated by the law forbidding physical punishment.

When the law of man is contrary to the law of God what must one do? The disciples faced this issue in the early days of the church. In Acts, chapter four, we are told that the Sanhedrin, addressing Peter and John, commanded them not to speak or teach at all in the name of Jesus."

"But Peter and John answered and said to them,

'Whether it is right in the sight of God to give heed to you rather than to God, you be the judge; for we cannot stop speaking what we have seen and heard' '' (Acts 4:19-20).

These apostles did not react in a spirit of rebellion. They were respectful of the human authority, but had no other alternative than to obey the command of the Lord to preach and heal. This is the pattern for us to follow. We must obey God rather than man and have faith that God will protect us or else give us the grace to bear the repercussions.

The rod CAN be misused, and physical and emotional injury to the child CAN occur. This does not mean that the use of the rod for discipline is wrong and should be abandoned. It rather means that parents must be taught the proper use of the rod. Spanking a child does not constitute child abuse. Any authority that so decrees has taken a position contrary to the Word of God. This should not intimidate the parent who respects God's Word and truly loves his children. Punishment is a necessary facet of bringing up children in the nurture of the Lord.

Effective rod ministry must be:

1. *Consistent:* The child must receive correction each time it is needed. If the parent spanks his child on some occasions of disobedience and not on others, the child can only be confused. Such a child cannot possibly learn obedience. The parent's inconsistency leaves him in frustration. It takes a disciplined parent to discipline a child. The undisciplined child is not to be blamed, but, the parents. A child's behavior is determined by parental love, care, instruction and punishment. Whenever the parent is inconsistent with discipline, this must be corrected before the child can learn proper respect and obedience.

"He who spares his rod hates his son, But he who loves him disciplines him diligently" (Proverbs 13:24).

2. *Timely:* The King James translation reads, "chasteneth him betimes" (Proverbs 13:24). The Hebrew word "shachar,"

141

betimes, means "to seek early." The early discipline of children has two applications. First, the child must be disciplined early in life. The training in obedience must begin in infancy. Second, the discipline must be proximate to the offense. The child must be able to relate the punishment to the cause; otherwise, he misses the point as to why he is spanked.

3. *Fair:* The punishment must be in keeping with the offense. There should be degrees of punishment. Was the child's offense major or minor? A rule book cannot be drawn up to regulate how many licks to give a child for certain offenses. This is because children are different in temperament. Some are corrected with much less discipline than others. The parent in any given situation must judge the degree of punishment needed, and his judgment must be fair. Excessive punishment is as damaging as no punishment.

4. *In Love:* Unless the punishment is seen by the child as an act of parental love, the results will be negative. Resentment and rebellion will be formed in his heart. Forgiveness and acceptance are manifestations of love. Once the punishment is finished, the atmosphere should be clear and normal love relationship between parent and child should prevail. Unless this is done, the child will identify correction as rejection, and the pattern will be carried into adult life.

Satan will take full advantage of any deviations from these standards of proper rod discipline. The parent that is deficient or unbalanced in the administration of proper discipline should make it a priority to change. The future happiness and well-being of the child is at stake.

The Book of Proverbs is a rich source of Divine wisdom on the subject of child discipline. Underline the following passages in your Bible and meditate upon them until their truths are in your heart:

Proverbs 10:13: "A rod is for the back of him who lacks

understanding." The rod helps a child to learn. He must be taught to understand right from wrong and good from evil. Strict discipline makes a child sensible to his faults. Note: The "back" should not be taken to mean the spine, but rather the back end of the child. Spinal injury can result from striking a child on his back.

Proverbs 13:24: "He who spares his rod hates his son, But he who loves him disciplines him diligently." This is addressed to parents. Discipline is the duty of parents, in particular the father. Discipline is an expression of love. The parent who neglects discipline shows that he does not really care about his child's welfare, for he has abandoned him to sin and Satan.

Proverbs 20:30: "Stripes that would scour away evil, And strokes reach the innermost parts." Some children are very obstinate and firm punishment is necessary to curb their rebellious wills. This verse reveals that a bruise left in the flesh is not tantamount to abuse. Worldly wisdom is more concerned with the condition of the flesh than of the soul. Proper discipline administered in love for the good of the child has a cleansing effect. Only by the wisdom of God can we appreciate the character-building influence of a good spanking.

Proverbs 22:6: "Train up a child in the way he should go, Even when he is old he will not depart from it." Children require protection from sin and all snares. Look upon them as soldiers in training for the army of God, for so they are. "The way he should go" is the way of God. Instill in the hearts of children a love for God, His Word, His church and His ministry. Such a child will never be ensnared and made a prisoner of Satan. We have here a sure promise from God that "he will not depart" from the path of righteousness into the ways of ruin.

Proverbs 22:15: "Foolishness is bound up in the heart of a child; The rod of discipline will remove it far from him."

Foolishness is not merely "found" but "bound" in the heart of a child. He has an inclination to sin from which he needs deliverance. In foolishness of heart he consistently makes the wrong choices when left to himself. Wisdom is not inherited but comes by the process of learning the ways of God. Correction is the necessary cure for folly. Gentle techniques are ineffective; the rod is necessary. Rashness and carelessness are symptoms of foolishness. The wise parent will not permit these traits to remain but will, through the rod ministry, remove them far from the child.

Proverbs 23:13-14: "Do not hold back discipline from the child, Although you beat him with the rod, he will not die. You shall beat him with the rod, And deliver his soul from Sheol." Some parents hold back on discipline because it is so unpleasant. Truly, for the moment it is not joyous but grievous, yet the ultimate result is the peaceable fruit of righteousness. The child may scream and agonize as though he were being killed, but he is not dying. The child's over-reaction is a ploy, hopefully to deter the spanking by appealing to the emotions of the parent.

There is deliverance in discipline. The rod will turn a child from the path of self-destruction into the fruitful life of self-discipline. It is better for the body to suffer a little discomfort than for the soul to perish. Eternal consequences hinge on discipline. This is why it must be done and done right.

Proverbs 29:15: "The rod and reproof give wisdom, But a child who gets his own way brings shame to his mother." The goal of education is not only to gain knowledge but wisdom. Children must not only be told what is good and evil, but be corrected when they neglect to do good and choose to do evil. The parent has two powerful instruments with which to instill wisdom in the child: the rod and reproof. Reproof is given by words. Its synonyms are censure, warning, rebuke and chiding. If reproof does the job without the rod, then well and good. If reproof alone does not bring the child to wisdom, then the rod is needed. But the rod should never be used without reproof. A serious reprimand should accompany the spanking. As the child takes warning he gains wisdom.

This Scripture sounds a warning that a child must not be left to his own indulgences. His own inclinations will lead him to unruly behavior. He will develop bad habits and bad attitudes. The child that mother has cuddled will ultimately become a disgrace to the family and more than likely, abusive to the mother herself. God intended children to be a blessing, but unless they are brought to wisdom they will become a curse.

Proverbs 29:17: "Correct your son, and he will give you comfort; He will also delight your soul." Families can be needlessly harassed and vexed by the ill-mannered behavior of undisciplined children. Parents can end the day with frayed nerves, tired bodies and hoarse voices through contending with an unruly child. A few days of scriptural discipline will reverse this sad condition. When a child is brought to peace, the parents have peace.

The happy fruit of strict discipline is sweet indeed. How blessed to be free from concern over the welfare of one's children and to see the prospect of blessedness both in this world and the one to come.

Guidelines for Discipline

1. *Be definite:* The child should know exactly what you expect of him. The toddler must know that the stereo is a "No-no!" The teenaged daughter must clearly understand that you expect her to keep her room clean and orderly. Vagueness produces confusion.

2. *Follow through:* When you have taken a definite position, do not give ground. When the requirements are not met, then follow through with appropriate discipline. Be sure that both parents stay in agreement and support one another in the discipline. Otherwise, the child will play one against the other.

3. *Discipline in private:* Do not discipline the child in public or in the presence of others. Take him aside. Your aim is not to shame but to correct.

4. *Reprove:* Explain the offense so that there will be no misunderstanding as to what the wrongdoing was and why it was wrong. Warn him of the consequences of his wrongdoing. Then put the responsibility for good conduct onto the child. Let him know that you do not intend to warn him over and over again.

5. *Keep your spirit right:* Do not punish a child in anger or for revenge. Discipline is not a time for the parent to vent his anger and frustration, but a time to correct the child.

6. *Be firm and thorough:* Spank hard enough and long enough to get the desired results. Be sure the correction has reached the child's heart. A quick slap, jerk, yell or pinch cannot achieve the goal. Do it God's way; use the rod.

7. *Require the child to receive punishment gracefully:* Do not permit him to twist away from you, fall on the floor or put his hands behind him.

8 *Let him cry:* Permit him to release his emotions. True repentance is usually accompanied by tears. Stay with him until the crying has ended. Note: If the child remains pouting, sullen, hateful or defiant, then the punishment is not complete.

9. *Establish forgiveness:* It is time to pray. Lead the child to ask God's forgiveness for his offense. Then you forgive the child and tell him so.

10. *Love the child:* You have not rejected the child but corrected him. Love him with hugs and kisses. One of the worst wounds that can be inflicted is rejection, but love builds security and motivates good behavior.

Note: There are some instances where parents have told us that they did all of these ten things and the child would not respond to the punishment. This points out the importance of ministering deliverance along with the punishment. Spanking deals with the flesh while deliverance is needed to drive out evil spirits.

Loving Children

Love is absolutely essential to the healthy development of personality. The root of ALL personality disturbance is rejection. So children require love — lots of love. This love should begin at conception. It actually makes a difference in one's life as to whether he was conceived in love or lust. This is because evil spirits can enter through the door of lust conception. Through deliverance, we have seen many set free from this curse.

A baby can receive love while still being carried in the mother's body. An embryo is no mere thing, but a living human being capable of receiving love. Even writers on prenatal care, writing from a natural observation rather than a spiritual one, have expressed the conviction that a baby knows whether or not he is loved from at least four month's development in the mother's womb. John the Baptist was filled with the Holy Spirit "while yet in his mother's womb" (Luke 1:15). So, the unborn child can be ministered to in love by the Spirit of God.

There are currently some healthy trends within the medical profession pertaining to father assisted births. Fathers-to-be are given a course of instruction and encouraged to participate in the birthing experience. The mother and father are permitted to hold and fondle the child immediately after birth. They are permitted to massage the vernix into the baby's skin. Instead of being isolated from the newborn infant, the baby is bonded to his parents through the intimacies of touching love. These trends are to be applauded and encouraged. It has been proven through a study of case histories that such babies develop into more secure, happy and stable personalities than others who are deprived of these intimacies.

God is love, and those who are partakers of the Divine nature can minister that love. The richest inheritance parents can give their children is the inheritance of godly love.

It takes time and patience to love children. Loving children must be made a priority, or other things will steal the time and opportunity. Father may be trying to relax and read the newspaper when his little son comes in with a newly discovered bug. Either that father has time and patience for little boys with little bugs; or, a few years later, that same son will be bugging his father in many ways.

Loving parents will be good listeners. Listen to what your children talk about. Get interested in their interests. Children should be able to talk to their parents about anything and everything. Communication may not seem so important when a child is young, but as he grows older the importance of communication is seen. The time to establish good communication is from early childhood. It is rarely developed in later years. Without communication, parental influence is lost.

Love is concerned with the total welfare of the child. Love makes every effort to protect the child physically, emotionally, mentally and spiritually. Every door must be guarded continuously against harm. The devil as a roaring lion goes about seeking whom he may devour. Little children are especially vulnerable. They are unable to protect themselves, and are totally dependent upon parents as guardians from all hurts.

Which is more important, a man's gold watch or his son's mind? What father would permit someone to open his watch and fill it with dirt? A man will protect his watch. Even greater protection should be provided for his son's mind. Unregulated television pours dirt into children's minds. Many evil spirits being cast out of children have gained their entrance through television. The entertaining and seemingly

148

harmless cartoons are prime offenders. Children are filled with fear as their little cartoon friends are splattered, smashed, torn apart, and tortured by ceaseless methods. Have you watched little children watch the cartoons? Have you observed the gamut of emotions they experience? Witchcraft and occult spirits enter readily through little children's curiosity and interest in satanic supernaturalism portrayed over these programs. Even the commercials stir little hearts to lust for material things. When little Susie goes to the store with mommy she cries, kicks and pouts until she gets the corny cereal or artificial fruit drink she saw advertised on television.

Little children cannot distinguish between fantasy and reality. We now have a whole generation raised on TV fantasies, many of whom are unable to cope with the realities of life. The heavy diet of fantasies has weakened their personalities. A fantasy is a lie, a deception. It is not the truth. Remember lies and deception are Satan's tools — not God's. Jesus is truth not a lie. God's Word is truth — not deception. "And you shall know the truth, and the truth shall make you free" (John 8:32). Lies lead to bondage, but truth shall make one free. So, our children need truth and not the lies and deception of fantasies.

A word study of "fantasy" is most revealing. It is a synonym of "fancy" which Webster defines as "a product of imagination, specif., an image; esp., an illusory image; phantasm." Thus, fantasy (fancy, phantasm) is "a figment of the disordered mind; a deceptive or illusory appearance (of something); a ghost."

In other words, fantasy is the deceptive work of a spirit, and that spirit is not the Holy Spirit for He is not a liar and a deceiver. The Holy Spirit is the inspirer of Scripture, none of which is fantasy and unreality, but absolute truth. The Greek word for "truth" (aletheia) means "actual, true to fact, real, genuine." Nowhere in Scripture does the Holy Spirit use fantasy as a vehicle to convey truth. The reason is clear: how can lies and deception become companions to truth or become a means to reveal truth?

Jesus at the age of twelve amazed the learned teachers in the temple with His insight into Scripture. Jesus was growing in "wisdom and stature, and in favor with God and men" (Luke 2:52), but not by watching Mickey Mouse on televison! His stability and strength of personality and character were the result of His involvement with truth.

The world, whose god is Satan, makes parents feel guilty if they deprive their children of fantasy. The parent, intent upon protecting children, must regularly discern the spirit of truth and the spirit of error. In speaking of the spirits of antichrist John declares:

> "They are from the world; therefore they speak as from the world, and the world listens to them. We are from God; he who knows God listens to us; he who is not from God does not listen to us. By this we know the spirit of truth and the spirit of error" (I John 4:5-6).

Children are little people; they soon grow up to be big people. The kind of people they become depends upon the dedication and commitment of their parents. Parents, God has given us the responsibility to teach, train, discipline and love our children. If we do not feel qualified, God will help us. It will require the best of us, but the rewards will be rich and eternal.

Kingdom living is worth all the effort that it takes. Everything outside of God's Kingdom is darkness and death. Dedicate yourselves to God and commit yourselves to Kingdom living for yourselves and your children.

> "Thanks be to God, who gives us the victory through our Lord Jesus Christ. Therefore . . . be steadfast immovable, always abounding in the work of the Lord, knowing that your toil is not in vain in the Lord" (I Corinthians 15:57-58).

Parent's Prayer

Lord, I accept the responsibility You have given to me to bring up my children in Your nurture and admonition. I recognize that You have made me a steward over my children. All that are mine are Yours. I seek Your approval as a good and faithful servant. I dedicate myself to You and set myself apart to Your glory. I sanctify myself by Your Word that my children may also be sanctified in truth.

Grant to me wisdom that I might accurately discern all things. Give me courage to do Your will in the face of all opposition. Give me love that I might lay down my life for my own as You laid down Your life for the church. Wherever I am ignorant, give me light and understanding and I will embrace it. Wherever I am in error, reveal it to me and I will replace it with truth. Wherever I have failed, grant me Your mercy. Wherever I am in error, reveal it to me and I will replace it with truth. Wherever I have failed, grant me Your mercy. Wherever I have sinned, grant me forgiveness.

I confess my own inability to carry out Your commission to me as a parent apart from Your strength. Without You I can do nothing, but through You, Lord, I can do all things because You strengthen me.

Show me where Satan has gained any access to my life that he might be renounced and cast out. Show me where Satan has gained access to my children that in Your name they might be delivered. Teach me how to protect my children from the evil one.

Lord, this family exists to serve You and to do Your will. I dedicate these children to Your glory. Together we acknowledge You as Lord. It is our prayer that we might always serve together in Your Kingdom. Grant us Your promised blessings of righteousness, peace and joy in the Holy Spirit. Amen.

CHAPTER X

Building and Battling

— OR A CHURCH [handwritten]

A family enjoying the peace and security of Kingdom living is like a city surrounded by massive walls. Each family member is like a section of stones set in the wall of Kingdom living. The stronger each stone, the stronger the wall. The stronger the wall, the greater the security from the enemy.

Walls do not "happen;" they are the product of arduous labor. It takes much hard work to build a home, to shape relationships with one another, to fulfill one's God-ordained function as a family member and to bring one's life into conformity with God's Word.

As you work at building your home, think of it as building a wall. You are first of all responsible for your portion of the wall. A family [*CHURCH* handwritten] is no stronger than its weakest member. Your section of the wall would look something like this:

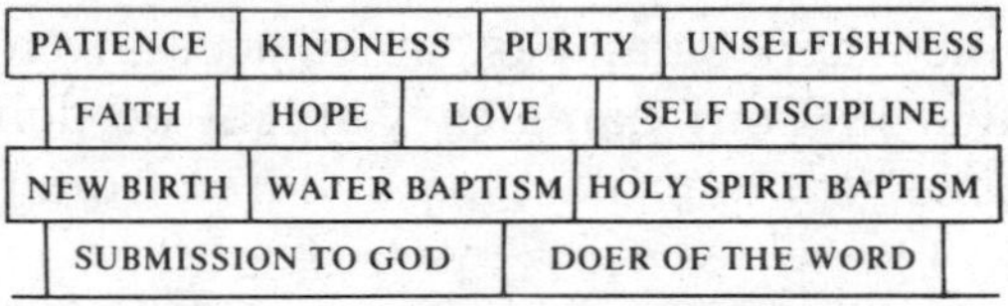

PATIENCE	KINDNESS	PURITY	UNSELFISHNESS
FAITH	HOPE	LOVE	SELF DISCIPLINE
NEW BIRTH	WATER BAPTISM	HOLY SPIRIT BAPTISM	
SUBMISSION TO GOD		DOER OF THE WORD	

Your Section of the Wall

The enemy can gain entrance through any breach or weak place in the wall. Satan, the roaring lion, is always roaming about looking for a way to get into the family and devour it. The wall must not only be built but maintained.

Whenever one family member is out of God's will, the whole family is vulnerable. The breach in the wall must be guarded. The watchmen must remain vigilant. Intercessors must fill any gaps created by other's failures. The other family members must be prepared to fight a spiritual warfare. The enemy will press to get in. Until the breach is closed, the rest must fend off the foe.

It is easy to become provoked at the one who has failed his position in the wall. This is what the enemy hopes will happen. When others react in a wrong way, he gains greater access to that family.

Even when the wall is intact and strong, the watchmen must be alert. The enemy will move in his battering ram and begin to tear at the wall. If he finds strife, confusion or pressure, he will have found a weak place in the wall.

In the days of Nehemiah the walls of Jerusalem lay in ruins. Sin had opened the way that led to Israel's captivity. There had been many casualties. Nehemiah had a burden. Something had to be done, and he was willing to be used of God. He saw the broken-down walls as a reproach to God. He saw the intimidations of the enemy as a challenge to believe God. He exhorted each family to battle. He met the fears of the people with a call to remember the greatness of God and to fight for their families.

> "When I saw their fear, I rose and spoke to the nobles, the officials, and the rest of the people, Do not be afraid of them; remember the Lord who is great and awesome, and fight for your brothers, your sons, your daughters, your wives, and your houses" (Nehemiah 4:14).

The enemy is not going away. He has no intention of ceasing his attacks. The devil considers the family a choice prize to capture. The family is in great peril today. Many have already met destruction, and others are shaken. But there is a way for victory over the devil. There is hope. We must all be aroused. We must remember the help we have in God and fight for ourselves and for one another. The alternative confronting us is the ruin and grief of destruction and bondage. If the family fails, the domino effect will see the church and the nation weakened to ineffectiveness.

A Pattern for Family Action
(A study of Nehemiah, Chapter Four)

"Now it came about that when Sanballat heard that we were rebuilding the wall, he became furious and very angry and mocked the Jews" (v.1). The enemy of the family must be identified and overcome. He is the same enemy who threatened the families in Nehemiah's day. He worked through a man named Sanballat who is typical of Satan himself. The name "Sanballat" literally means "a fallen branch." His name represents one who was created beautiful but became a fallen one. How descriptive of Satan who was once called Lucifer, the morning star. He was the most beautiful of God's created angels and bore the highest place in God's presence. (See Ezekiel 28:11-15.) But he became filled with pride, led a rebellion in heaven against God and was cast out. Jesus declared, "I was watching Satan fall from heaven like lightning" (Luke 10:18). Isaiah reports Satan's fall with these words, "How you have fallen from heaven, O star of the morning, son of the dawn" (Isaiah 14:12). It is the same enemy that we face today whom Nehemiah faced then. He has not changed his target nor his tactics.

When Sanballat saw the restoration of the walls under way he was "very angry." Why was he so angry? Because he had enjoyed ready access to Jerusalem. As long as the walls were down, he could enter at will and could keep the people there under his control. The walls meant an end to his domination. SAINTS W/O BAPHS + TRUTH - DEEPER

Indeed, the enemy of Kingdom living is disturbed when he sees the walls of protection going up around a family. He is the only one who has anything to lose. Jerusalem could never be a strong city as long as its walls were down. The same is true of my family and yours. Each family member bears his share of responsibility by maintaining his place in God, for we are warned by God's word:

"Like a city that is broken into and without walls is a man

154

who has no control over his spirit" (Proverbs 25:28).

Sanballat takes up his first form of attack. He "mocked" those who purposed in their hearts to rebuild the walls, and he will do the same toward us. He will seek to melt our newly formed resolutions with a blast of doubt. "Who do you think you are? What do you hope to accomplish?" Can you stand strong in the face of the enemy's belittling? Will you persevere even in the face of mockery and strengthen your life in God.

> "And he spoke in the presence of his brothers and the wealthy men of Samaria and said, 'What are these feeble Jews doing? Are they going to restore it for themselves? Can they offer sacrifices? Can they finish in a day? Can they revive the stones from the dusty rubble even the burned ones?' " (Nehemiah 4:2).

Sanballat is meeting privately with his counselors. Yet God is revealing to Nehemiah every word spoken in the secret chambers of the enemy. Oh, Saints, we have a heavenly wiretap into Satan's headquarters. We can know all that Satan is plotting against our families.

There was a time when the King of Aram was warring against Israel. The king of Israel knew this king's every move, because God revealed it to his prophet, Elisha. The king of Aram thought there was a traitor in his camp, so he confronted his soldiers: "Will you tell me which of us is for the king of Israel?" And one of his servants said, "No, my lord, O king; but Elisha, the prophet who is in Israel, tells the king of Israel the words that you speak in your bedroom" (See II Kings 6:8-12).

As Paul said concerning Satan, "We are not ignorant of his schemes" (II Corinthians 2:11). God will reveal to us every plot and plan that Satan devises against us. This is how we will defeat Satan in his gates; the place of his private counsel against us. He cannot deceive us into warring against flesh and blood, for we will know who the real enemy is, and we will wrestle triumphantly against the principalities

155

and powers in the heavenlies.

We should be more aware of what we can do to the devil. We need to get it in our hearts that Satan trembles when God's people begin to move in obedience to God. He fears the family that is moving into Divine order and function.

Sanballat gathers his cohorts for a pep rally. He is trying to encourage himself by asking a series of questions. The enemy is trying to convince himself that God's people cannot succeed:

"What are these feeble Jews doing?" He calls them "feeble Jews." He is trying to convince himself that they are feeble. Then he will try to convince the Jews themselves that they are feeble. But they are not feeble! They are God's children, heirs of the promises. They are fulfilling prophecy in God's timing. God said they could return from captivity and rebuild their walls. And He has said the same for us. We are not feeble in Christ. "But you are a chosen race, a royal priesthood, a holy nation, a people for God's own possession, that you may proclaim the excellencies of Him who has called you out of darkness into His marvelous light" (I Peter 2:9).

Has Satan convinced you that you are feeble? He so convinced the Israelites at times when they were at the very point of triumph. There was a day when Israel was ready to enter into the glorious inheritance of Canaan. Those who spied out the land testified that it was indeed a land of milk and honey. But ten of the twelve spies saw only the strength of the enemy. Their eyes were no longer upon God and His promises. They said,

> "We are not able to go up against the people, for they are too strong for us . . . All the people whom we saw in it are of great size . . . and we became like grasshoppers in our own sight, and so we were in their sight" (Numbers 13:31-33).

Our inheritance is before us. Our God exhorts us to take the land, to fight for our brothers, our sons, our daughters, our wives, our households. Our Lord says, "Build the walls. I desire that you live in security and peace." If we go on to victory we must see ourselves as able in the Lord, not as grasshoppers.

"Are they going to restore it for themselves?" questions Sanballat. The old serpent tries to convince himself and us that God will not help: we will have to do it all by ourselves. Satan does not want us to believe that any family can be restored. He is sitting on the ruins. The judgment of God upon their sins has given him a legal right to perpetuate their misery. "True, Satan, our problems are due to sin — ours and our forefathers — but you have forgotten the grace of God. Our God is merciful to sinners."

> "He will not always strive with us; Nor will He keep His anger forever. He has not dealt with us according to our sins, Nor rewarded us according to our iniquities.
> For as high as the heavens are above the earth, So great is His lovingkindness toward those who fear Him. As far as the east is from the west, So far has He removed our transgressions from us" (Psalm 103:9-12).

But "can they offer sacrifices?" Satan fears above all things that sinners be restored to their worship of God. The Jews had not worshipped God in their temple for seventy years. Surely this will not be restored to them. Satan's aim is to cut us off from God. The greatest evidence that he has lost the battle for a family is when that family begins to worship the Father "in spirit and truth" (John 4:23).

The Old Testament sacrifices spoke prophetically of the redemptive work of Christ. They represented the blessings accruing in the cross to all who believe. Satan is worried. Will those whom he has robbed so long now be restored to the fullness of their blessings in the Lord?

"Can they finish in a day?" Can there be a quick restoration of that which has been in ruins so long? Actually, the walls of Jerusalem were restored in record time. This massive task was accomplished in only fifty-two days. It was not merely a natural work of man but a supernatural work of

God. How was it accomplished? The context reveals that every one had a mind to work; they worked in unity under God's direction. They were submitted to the authorities placed over them by God. They were set in array. —

The devil tries to pressure us with time, as he did Nehemiah. He will remind us of how long we have sought for solutions. His aim is to make us feel hopeless and give up. His thoughts begin to bombard our minds, "Why don't you quit trying? You know it's not going to work out. You haven't seen any signs of change yet, have you?"

As long as one knows God is with him, and that his hope is in the Father, he has strength to endure. At times of stress and pressure, we must stand on the Rock. Obedience to God's Word will see us through the storms of life.

> "Therefore everyone who hears these words of mine, and acts upon them, may be compared to a wise man, who built his house upon a rock. And the rain descended, and the floods came, and the winds blew, and burst against that house; and yet it did not fall, for it had been founded upon the rock" (Matthew 7:24-25).

When you sense that time is running out, and you see family conditions going from bad to worse in spite of your prayers, the devil will rob you of peace and overwhelm you with fear unless you agree with the God who is not limited by either time or circumstance.

> "Consider it all joy, my brethren, when you encounter various trials, knowing that the testing of your faith produces endurance. And let endurance have its perfect result, that you may be perfect, lacking in nothing" (James 1:2-4).

You may be a broken and burned stone yourself. Or it may be your companion or your own child that is in need of restoration. Is anything too hard for the Lord? Turn your eyes upon Jesus. "For truly I say unto you, if you have faith as a mustard seed, you shall say to this mountain, 'Move from here to there,' and it shall move; and nothing shall be impossible to you" (Matthew 17:20).

"Now Tobiah the Ammonite was near him and he said, 'Even what they are building — if a fox should jump on it, he would break their stone wall down' " (Nehemiah 4:3). Tobiah stands beside Sanballat to support him. Tobiah's name means "God is good." His name is one of mockery. Tobiah represents one of Satan's strong men who comes to question men in trials as to the goodness of God. He querries, "If your God is so good, then why has He permitted all this evil? Why has He stood aloof and let all these evils beset your family? Why? Why? Why?" Oh, how Tobiah would have us blame God; for the one who accuses God has abandoned his true source of help. The devil has always accused God, and whoever sides with accusing God has become the devil's assistant.

Then Tobiah continues hell's pep rally. The devil and his demons often think they have everything in the bag. How could their plans possibly go awry? But we must remember the cross and the resurrection. Satan just knew his great strategy to defeat Christ had succeeded. He had not succeeded in getting Jesus to submit to him, but he had now murdered Jesus. "The battle is won!" he thought. However, the very thing that he thought gave him victory was the thing that defeated him. If he had known that his plan would backfire, he would never have crucified the Lord of glory. (See I Corinthians 2:6-8.)

The demons still try to assure themselves that our families are hopelessly bound and unable to rebuild their walls. Tobiah said, "Even what they are building — if a fox should jump on it, he would break their stone wall down" (v. 3).

The enemy is boasting: "Husband, wife, son or daughter — it will not take much to overthrow your puny efforts at family restoration. All we have to do is send one little fox (only one small demon) and he will break down all you think you have achieved." He will put any thought he can into our minds to discourage us. We must defeat him with the sword of the Spirit which is the Word of God. When he tells us of our weakness, we will remind him of our strength in God. "I can do all things through Him who strengthens me" (Philippians 4:13). We are strong in the Lord and in the strength of His might. When we put on the full armor of God, we are able to stand firm against the schemes of the devil. (See Ephesians 6:10-11.)

In verses four and five Nehemiah prays, "Hear, O our God, how we are despised." The "we" includes God. When we are despised for standing in faith and obedience toward God, then God is also despised. Any attack upon God's child is an attack upon God. We must know that we are not alone in our battle. We are no match for the devil within ourselves — BUT GOD!!

What a strange prayer Nehemiah prayed. Listen to it:

> "Return their reproach on their own heads and give them up for plunder in a land of captivity. Do not forgive their iniquity and let not their sin be blotted out before Thee, for they have demoralized the builders" (v. 4-5).

In effect, Nehemiah prays, "Lord, let their plan against us backfire. Let the ruin planned for us come upon them." We are not required to have sympathy for the devil. We can pray that Satan's plans against us will result in his own destruction. Again, this is exactly what happened when Satan crucified Jesus. Satan's tactic against Jesus resulted in his own defeat. His attacks upon the family can turn its members to repentance and faith. A family can be turned to unity through Satan's efforts to tear it apart. Lord, let the enemy overplay his hand.

Nehemiah was praying, too, for God's intervention. His conscience was clear, and he could come boldly before God's throne. There are times when God's intervention is the only salvation for us or our family. God's sovereign intervention can save us as it saved Israel from the wrath of Pharaoh at the Red Sea. Moses was confident of God's help. He said to the families of Israel:

"Do not be afraid! Stand by and see the salvation of the Lord which He will accomplish for you today; for the Egyptians whom you have seen today, you will never see them again forever. The Lord will fight for you while you keep silent" (Exodus 14:13-14).

The Red Sea opened and God's people crossed on dry ground. Then the waters overwhelmed the pursuing Egyptian army.

If it requires a miracle of grace to save us, our God is able. When you have been obedient in all that is shown you, then pray and stand in faith.

"So we built the wall and the whole wall was joined together to half its height, for the people had a mind to work" (Nehemiah 4:6). This is the priority. Satan will do everything in his power to divert us from building our own spiritual life as a segment of the family wall. He must stop our development of disciplined living, faith, love, sanctification and unity. Some individuals and families stay so busy fighting brush fires that they never get anything else done. Thus, they are diverted from building. It is possible to so occupy ourselves with Satan's intimidations that we are diverted from the main task of building the wall. When we are diverted, Satan has accomplished his purpose.

It is possible to get too occupied with the devil — even with our victories over him. When the seventy disciples returned from a few days of ministry, they were exuberant over their ability to cast out demons. They rejoiced in that "even the demons are subject to us in Your name." Jesus replied, "Do not rejoice in this, that the spirits are subject to you, but rejoice that your names are recorded in heaven" (Luke 10:17,20). The important thing is our relationship with God.

"And the whole wall was joined together to half its height" (Nehemiah 4:6). Every breach in the wall received attention. The wall was built partially all the way around the city. It was not as high as it would be eventually, but every foot of the wall experienced partial restoration. This is

161

an example for us. The devil may have been getting into our families through such breaches as resentment, hurt, jealousy, rebellion, pride, carelessness, selfishness and criticism. All of these breaches must be sealed up in the Lord. Instead of working on each hole in the wall separately until they are brought up to standard, one should work on all the gaps at one time and bring the wall up at least half way. This in itself is a major accomplishment. It affords some protection from enemy attacks. To complete even this much we must have a "mind to work." But we must not settle for a half-built wall. The commitment to finish the job must be resolved in our hearts, and the building continue until it is completed.

When the entire federation of enemy powers "heard that the repair of the walls of Jerusalem went on, and the breaches began to be closed, they were very angry" (Nehemiah 4:7). The only way Satan can defeat anyone is through division. His basic plan is to divide and conquer. He conquers nations, churches and families by division. Wherever there are breaches in relationships, Satan can get in. When the breaches of relationships are healed, Satan is filled with angry frustration.

As the individual family member repairs his portion of the wall, and the ones next to him repair theirs, the net result is the closing of the breaches among themselves. It is essential to keep the wall intact. Any breach in relationships becomes the priority for our prompt attention. Repentance by the offender and forgiveness by the offended close the gap as reconciliation takes place, and unity is restored. We can know the importance of family unity from the fact of Satan's fierce hatred of it.

"And all of them conspired together to come and fight against Jerusalem and to cause a disturbance in it" (v. 8). Here we learn two important facts about the devil. First, he does not give up. He may lose one round, but he comes back for another. When Satan, the tempter, was defeated by Jesus in their wilderness encounter, the Scripture says,

162

"he departed from him until an opportune time" (Luke 4:13).

Second, we are told that the enemy "conspired together." There is unity in the satanic kingdom. Jesus observed the unity of Satan and his demons when he taught us that Satan's kingdom is not divided against itself. (See Matthew 12:24-26.) What holds them in such unity? To be sure, it is not the unity of love such as prevails in God's Kingdom. No, satanic unity is founded on hatred and fear. The demons have one thing in common: an unfathomable hatred for God and for man, and a fear of failing their master, Satan.

The enemy's conspiracy was designed to fight against Jerusalem and cause a disturbance in it. The Hebrew word for "disturbance" means *injury, confusion and failure.* This is what Satan will cause in a family without walls. This amplification of "disturbance" is progressive. First, there is *injury* where the family members yield to unkindness and hurt one another through rejection, neglect or abuse. Then comes *confusion* through distrust, retaliation, rebellion and almost always from a breakdown in communication. The end result is *failure* — either the failure of the family to function as a unit in God's Kingdom or to actually disintegrate and be permanently torn apart.

"But we prayed unto our God, and because of them we set up a guard against them day and night" (Nehemiah 4:9). The prayers must continue. We must stay in touch with God so that we can move in His counsel and receive the strength of His presence. In a time of family crisis there are two imminent temptations: fear and flesh.

On the eve of His crucifixion Jesus and His disciples came to Gethsemane. Satan was poised for his attack. Jesus went to prayer. He also alerted the eleven with him saying, "Keep watch with me." A few minutes later he found them all asleep and awakened them saying, "Keep watching and praying that you may not enter into temptation; the spirit is willing but the flesh is weak" (Matthew 26:38-42).

Once again the disciples fell asleep, and when the tempter came, they were unprepared. The flesh took over and

Peter grabbed his sword and cut off a man's ear. When Jesus negated his fleshly weapon (v. 52), Peter was overtaken by fear and followed at a distance (v. 58). Because of fear he then denied his Lord (v. 70). All this was the result of not having prayed in the time of opportunity.

When the family is under attack it is not the time to sleep, but to set a prayer watch day and night. Fear is especially active at night.

> "So then let us not sleep as others do, but let us be alert and sober. For those who sleep do their sleeping at night, and those who get drunk get drunk at night. But since we are of the day, let us be sober, having put on the breastplate of faith and love, and as a helmet, the hope of salvation" (I Thessalonians 5:6-8).

"Thus, in Judah it is said, 'The strength of the burden bearers is failing, yet there is much rubbish; And we ourselves are unable to rebuild the wall' " (Nehemiah 4:10). This is what is called a bad confession. What has happened since verse six where Judah "had a mind to work?" The task was greater than they had judged. It can be accurately assessed that Judah had grown weary in well-doing and was in danger of losing the victory. They had grown tired from the clean-up operation and yet much rubbish remained.

Before the family can build the wall, it must first remove the rubbish. The rubbish represents all the bad attitudes, resentments, prejudices, wrong habit patterns of thought, speech and behavior, and every residue of sin. Most of us are truly surprised at how much rubbish there is when we really start digging into it. It takes genuine honesty and humility on the part of each one to face up to his personal share of rubbish. Usually, we are deceived into thinking all the garbage belongs to others. We must each stand before the mirror of God's Word and see ourselves as we truly are. Once we have seen ourselves, we must be diligent to work at the clean-up until it is finished.

"Therefore putting aside all filthiness and all that remains of wickedness, in humility receive the word implanted, which is able to save your souls. But prove yourselves doers of the word, and not merely hearers who delude themselves. For if anyone is a hearer of the word and not a doer, he is like a man who looks at his natural face in a mirror; for once he has looked at himself and gone away, he has immediately forgotten what kind of person he was. But one who looks intently at the perfect law, the law of liberty, and abides by it, not having become a forgetful hearer but an effectual doer, this man shall be blessed in what he does" (James 1:21-25).

So, the key to successful clean-up is spelled P-E-R-S-I-S-T-E-N-C-E.

How ironic that Judah should become discouraged. Judah means "praise." The power of praise is manifest in the strength it supplies for endurance. Judah was no longer living up to his name. Praise prevents and overcomes discouragement. Praise rivets our hearts and minds upon the Lord. As we praise Him, we become aware of what a mighty God we serve. Though the task be long and hard, we find God's Word is true again: "For the joy of the Lord is your strength" (Nehemiah 8:10b).

"And our enemies said, 'They will not know or see until we come among them, kill them, and put a stop to the work' " (v. 11). As soon as Judah made a bad confession, the enemy had something to say! The devil knows when our attention is off God and onto our problems. When we confess our doubts and our fears, it is the moment for which he has been waiting. Now he can initiate his blitz. He boasts that he will overcome us before we know what hit us.

Then Judah's discouragement was compounded by their relatives. "And it came about when the Jews who lived near them came and told us ten times, 'They will come up against us from every place where you may turn' " (v. 12). These relatives were those who had remained in Jerusalem when the others were taken away into captivity. Surely, they were authorities on not restoring the walls, for they had lived among the rubble for seventy years without setting one stone in place. We need not be swayed by the negativism of ungodly counsel even if it is repeated "ten times" by those of closest kin. The devil will use every available mouth to sow doubt and fear in our hearts.

"Then I stationed men in the lowest parts of the space behind the wall, the exposed places, and I stationed the people in families with their swords, spears and bows" (v. 13). Nehemiah observed that some places along the wall were more vulnerable than others. These "exposed places" were more carefully guarded. As you examine your part of the family wall, you will see that in some areas of your life you are more vulnerable to enemy attack than in others. For example, you may have a low tolerance for others' shortcomings. So impatience is a low place in your wall. This area of your life must be carefully guarded. Note your more vulnerable areas and be especially watchful.

Nehemiah further stationed the people in families with their weapons. Each family stood together against the common foe. Their energies were not consumed in conflict among themselves. Each person supported the others. They were all armed with the weapons provided. Success for any family is at hand when that family reaches such a point of unity as this in the employment of its spiritual weaponry against the devil.

"Those who were rebuilding the wall and those who carried burdens took their load with one hand doing the work and the other holding a weapon" (v. 17). Each builder worked with his hand on his weapon. Their goal was to finish the wall. Nothing could deter them. They refused to be stopped or sidetracked. If they should find it necessary to fight, then they were equipped and ready. In order to build they must be prepared to battle. Nehemiah and his builders never had to engage themselves in direct battle: some wall-builders do.

The enemies of the Jews were not annihilated; rather they remained close by and attempted other tactics. But Nehemiah and the people carefully followed the plans that God revealed to them. "So the wall was completed . . . and

166

it came about when all our enemies heard of it, and all the nations surrounding us saw it, they lost their confidence; for they recognized that this work had been accomplished with the help of our God" (Nehemiah 6:15-16).

These truths from Nehemiah give us encouragement and motivation. While our eyes are opened to the tactics of the devil to destroy us, they are also opened to the help we have in God. The family that finds itself with broken-down walls is offered a plan for restoration. We must not fear the enemy or be dismayed at the task confronting us, but begin to build and battle. The Lord is with us. BUILD + BATTLE

FAULTY PROTECTION

The Author's Prayer

Oh, Heavenly Father, we beseech you in behalf of families everywhere. The enemy is attacking the families as never before. They need to know that You have a plan for them whereby they can overcome the attacks of the enemy and come into their inheritance of Kingdom living. May the truths of Your Word which are shared in this book be quickened by the Holy Spirit to those who read them. Move upon family members to cooperate with Your Spirit's guidance in entering into the Divine order of husband's headship, wife's submission and children's obedience. Bring forth the Elijah ministry of family restoration that our nation may be spared your judgment! Strengthen our nation and our churches through the healing and restoration of our families. Amen.

Bestseller!!

PIGS IN THE PARLOR

$3.95

If you *really believe* JESUS delivered people from evil spirits . . . Then you owe it to yourself to read this book! Learn that it *still happens today!*

This book contains a wealth of practical information for the person **interested in, planning to engage in, or actively engaged in** the ministry of deliverance.

It is a PRACTICAL HANDBOOK, offering valuable guidance as to determining . . .

- **HOW DEMONS ENTER** ● **IF DELIVERANCE IS NEEDED** ● **HOW DELIVERANCE IS ACCOMPLISHED FOR OTHERS AND SELF** ● **HOW TO RETAIN DELIVERANCE** ● **GROUPINGS OF DEMONS** (listing those demons that are often found together).

The book also includes a chapter presenting a revelation on the problems of **SCHIZOPHRENIA** which could well revolutionize the way this subject has been traditionally viewed by the medical profession!

A BLOOD COVENANT
IS THE MOST
SOLEMN, BINDING AGREEMENT POSSIBLE
BETWEEN TWO PARTIES.

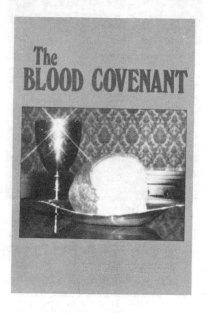

Perhaps one of the least understood, and yet most important and relevant factors necessary for an appreciation of the series of covenants and covenant relationships that our God has chosen to employ in His dealings with man, is the concept of the BLOOD COVENANT!

In this volume which has been "sold out," and "unavailable" for generations, lies truth which has blessed and will continue to bless every pastor, teacher, every serious Christian desiring to "go on with God."

Andrew Murray stated it beautifully years ago, when he said that if we were to but grasp the full knowledge of what God desires to do for us and understood the nature of His promises, it would "make the Covenant the very gate of heaven! May the Holy Spirit give us some vision of its glory."

$5.95

Alive Again!

**Bill Banks.
Terminal Cancer.
48 hours to live.**

Miraculously
healed!

The author, healed over twelve years ago, relates his own story. His own testimony presents a miracle or really a series of miracles—as seen through the eyes of a doubting skeptic, who himself becomes the object of the greatest miracle, because he is Alive Again!

The way this family pursues and finds divine healing as well as a great spiritual blessing provides a story that will at once bless you, refresh you, restore your faith or challenge it! You will not be the same after you have read this true account of the healing gospel of Jesus Christ, and how He is working in the world today.

The healing message contained in this book needs to be heard by every cancer patient, every seriously ill person, and by every Christian hungering for the reality of God.

More than a powerful testimony—here is teaching which can introduce you or those whom you love to healing and to a new life in the Spirit!

FRANK HAMMOND
Author of PIGS IN THE PARLOR: amplifies and expands the teachings of this important book in several series of cassettes. In these tapes he reveals additional truths gleaned from his own far-reaching ministry in the area of deliverance and related fields. Much, much needed truth and light to be gained from his right insights and down-to-earth teaching. (3.95 each)**

DELIVERANCE SERIES:
_____1. HEALING THE PERSONALITY
_____2. THE SCHIZOPHRENIA REVELATION (I)
_____3. THE SCHIZOPHRENIA REVELATION (II)
_____4. MAINTAINING DELIVERANCE
_____5. DEALING WITH PRESSURES
_____6. THE ARM OF FLESH

FREEDOM FROM BONDAGE SERIES:
_____1. ESCAPE INTO BONDAGE
_____2. BONDAGE TO SIN
_____3. BONDAGE TO SELF
_____4. BONDAGE TO MAN
_____5. BREAKING OF CURSES
_____6. FLESH VS. SPIRIT

FAITH SERIES:
_____1. THINGS THAT DESTROY FAITH
_____2. THINGS THAT ENCOURAGE FAITH
_____3. THE LANGUAGE OF FAITH
_____4. CORRESPONDING ACTION OF FAITH
_____5. THE DEVELOPMENT OF FAITH
_____6. PRAYING THE PRAYERS OF PAUL

END-TIME SERIES:
_____1. END-TIME BEHAVIOR (PART I)
_____2. END-TIME BEHAVIOR (PART II)
_____3. END-TIME BEHAVIOR (PART III)
_____4. END-TIME BEHAVIOR (PART IV)
_____5. THE CHRISTIAN & TRIBULATION
_____6. THE UNRIGHTEOUSNESS & GOD'S

MESSAGES ON LOVE SERIES:
_____1. FRIENDSHIP
_____2. MY BROTHER'S KEEPER
_____3. THE PERFECTING LOVE
_____4. LEARNING TO LOVE
_____5. REMEMBERING TO FORGET

WALK IN THE SPIRIT SERIES:
_____1. FUNCTIONING AS SPIRITUAL MEN
_____2. SPIRITUAL PERCEPTION
_____3. SEEING INTO THE SPIRITUAL REALM
_____4. THE FRUIT OF RIGHTEOUSNESS
_____5. WHAT ADVANTAGE MY RIGHTEOUSNESS
_____6. THE MINISTRY OF EDIFICATION

SPIRITUAL MEAT SERIES:
_____1. THE LORD'S SUPPER
_____2. DISCERNING THE LORD'S BODY
_____3. WORSHIP & PRAISE
_____4. WHAT DEFILES A MAN
_____5. "STABILIZE"
_____6. KNOWING WHO YOU ARE AS A BELIEVER

FAMILY IN THE KINGDOM SERIES:
_____1. THE HUSBAND'S HEADSHIP
_____2. THE WIFE'S SUBMISSION
_____3. THE WIFE'S INFLUENCE
_____4. BRINGING UP CHILDREN (PART I)
_____5. BRINGING UP CHILDREN (PART II)
_____6. THE WIFE'S SANTIFICATION (IDA MAE HAMMOND)

CHURCH SERIES:
_____1. THE BODY OF CHRIST
_____2. THE FAMILY OF GOD
_____3. THE TEMPLE OF GOD
_____4. GOD'S HUSBANDRY
_____5. THE ARMY OF GOD
_____6. THE BRIDE OF CHRIST

RECOGNIZING GOD SERIES:
_____1. GOD OUR SOURCE
_____2. GOD OUR PROVIDER
_____3. GOD OUR REFUGE

★ ★ ★ ★ ★ ★ ★ ★ ★ ★ ★ ★ **SPECIAL OFFERS** ★ ★ ★ ★ ★ ★ ★ ★ ★ ★ ★ ★
A) All 56 tapes listed above $170.00 (Save more than $50.00!)
B) Each 6 tape series Special Price only $19.75! (You pay for 5 tapes, 6th tape is FREE)
C) Buy any 12 tapes at $3.95 and you may choose 2 bonus tapes FREE of charge.

Write for our catalog of cassettes — listing tapes with brief description of each tape.

FOR THOSE SEEKING MORE INFORMATION..
...ABOUT DEMONOLOGY & DELIVERANCES

Banks, Bill
_____ MINISTERING TO THE AFTERMATH OF
ABORTION . . . . P   3.95 _____

Basham, Don
_____ DELIVER US FROM EVIL . . . . P   5.95 _____

_____ CAN A CHRISTIAN HAVE A DEMON . . . . P   1.25 _____

Garrison, Mary
_____ HOW TO TRY A SPIRIT . . . . P   3.95 _____

Gasson, Raphael
_____ CHALLENGING COUNTERFEIT . . . . P   1.95 _____

Hagin, Kenneth
Satan Demons, and Demon Possession Series
_____ VOL. 1-ORIGIN & OPERATION OF DEMONS . . . . . . P   1.00 _____

_____ VOL. 2-DEMONS & HOW TO DEAL WITH
THEM . . . . P   1.00 _____

_____ VOL. 3-MINISTERING TO THE OPPRESSED ...... P   1.00 _____

_____ VOL. 4-BIBLE ANSWERS/DEMONS.............. P   1.00 _____

Hammond, Frank & Ida Mae
_____ PIGS IN THE PARLOR .... P   3.95 _____

Lindsay, Gordon
_____ JOHN G. LAKE SERMONS ON DOMINION OVER
DEMONS, DISEASE, AND DEATH .... P   3.50 _____

_____ SATAN'S REBELLION AND FALL .... P   1.25 _____

_____ SATAN'S FALLEN ANGELS AND DEMONS....... P   1.25 _____

_____ SATAN'S DEMON MANIFESTATION .... P   1.25 _____

Manuel, Frances D.
_____ THOUGH AN HOST SHOULD ENCAMP.......... P   2.50 _____

Prince, Derek
_____ EXPELLING DEMONS .... P   .75 _____

_____ SERIES ON DELIVERANCE — ON CASSETTE TAPES —
_____ 6001 HOW I CAME TO GRIPS WITH DEMONS
_____ 6002 HOW JESUS DEALT WITH DEMONS
_____ 6003 NATURE AND ACTIVITY OF DEMONS
_____ 6004 HOW TO RECOGNIZE AND EXPEL DEMONS
_____ 6005 CULT AND OCCULT: SATAN'S SNARES DISCLOSED
_____ 6006 SEVEN WAYS TO KEEP YOUR DELIVERANCE
_____ 6007 TEENAGERS: YOUTH'S PLACE AND PROBLEMS IN THE
END TIME
_____ 6008 CHILDREN (5-11): INSTRUCTIONS ON DELIVERANCE FOR
CHILDREN AND THEIR PARENTS
_____ CASSETTES .... EACH   4.95 _____
_____ SET OF 6001-6006 ALBUM ...... SPECIAL   25.50 _____
_____ SET OF 8 ABOVE CASSETTES .... 34.50 _____

Ten Boom, Corrie
_____ DEFEATED ENEMIES .... P   1.25 _____

**(SAVE $11.85 — Entire Set of Above Books and Tapes ONLY $75.50
Save $6.25 All *Books Only* (No Tapes) ONLY $30.50)**

ABOUT THE ENEMY & OUR ROLE

Brant, Roxanne
_____ HOW TO TEST PROPHECY PREACHING,
AND GUIDANCE .... P   5.50 _____

Freeman, Hobart
_____ ANGELS OF LIGHT? .... P   2.95 _____

Hagin, Kenneth
_____ AUTHORITY OF THE BELIEVER .... P   1.00 _____

Harper, Michael
_____ SPIRITUAL WARFARE .... P   2.95 _____

King, Clarence
_____ GREATER IS HE .... P   1.25 _____

Mumford, Bob
_____ TAKE ANOTHER LOOK AT GUIDANCE .... P   4.95 _____

White, Anne
_____ TRIAL BY FIRE .... P   1.95 _____

(Save $3.00 — Entire Set of Above Books ONLY $17.55)

...about THE BAPTISM OF THE HOLY SPIRIT

Basham, Don
_____ HANDBOOK ON THE HOLY SPIRIT BAPTISM.... P   2.95 _____

_____ MINISTERING THE BAPTISM IN THE
HOLY SPIRIT (SPIRITUAL POWER) .... P   2.25 _____

Bennett, Dennis
_____ HOLY SPIRIT AND YOU .... P   4.95 _____

_____ NINE O'CLOCK IN THE MORNING .... P   4.95 _____

Banks, Bill
_____ ALIVE AGAIN! .... P   3.95 _____

Christenson, Larry
_____ SPEAKING IN TONGUES .... P   3.50 _____

Delgado, Gabriele
_____ A LOVE STORY.................................... P   1.25 _____

Gillies, George & Harriett
_____ SCRIPTURAL OUTLINE OF THE BAPTISM
IN THE HOLY SPIRIT .... P   1.00 _____

Hagin, Kenneth
_____ HOLY SPIRIT AND HIS GIFTS .... P   5.00 _____

_____ SEVEN VITAL STEPS TO RECEIVING THE
HOLY SPIRIT.................................... P   1.00 _____

Henley, Gary
_____ THE QUIET REVOLUTION .... P   4.95 _____

Lindsay, Gordon
SERIES ON GIFTS OF THE SPIRIT
_____ VOL. 1 .... P   2.50 _____
_____ VOL. 2 .... P   2.50 _____
_____ VOL. 3 .... P   2.50 _____
_____ VOL. 4 .... P   2.50 _____

Lensch, Rodney
_____ MY PERSONAL PENTECOST .... P   1.25 _____

Prince, Derek
_____ BAPTISM IN THE HOLY SPIRIT .... P   1.25 _____

Sherrill, John
_____ THEY SPEAK WITH OTHER TONGUES.......... P   2.95 _____

Tari, Mel as told to Cliff Dudley
_____ LIKE A MIGHTY WIND........................... P   2.95 _____

(Save $8.15 — Entire Set of Above Books ONLY $46.00)

...ABOUT HEALING FROM GOD
Banks, Bill
_____ ALIVE AGAIN! .... P   3.95 _____

_____ HOW I WAS HEALED OF CANCER & BAPTISED
WITH THE HOLY SPIRIT! 1 hr. cass. .... P   3.95 _____

Bosworth, F.F.
_____ CHRIST THE HEALER .... P   5.95 _____

Hagin, Kenneth
_____ HEALING BELONGS TO US .... P   1.00 _____

_____ KEYS TO SCRIPTURAL HEALING .... P   1.00 _____

Lindsay, Gordon
SERIES ON DIVINE HEALING AND HEALTH
_____ CHRIST THE GREAT PHYSICIAN .... P   1.00 _____

_____ HOW YOU CAN HAVE DIVINE HEALTH......... P   1.00 _____

_____ THE BIBLE SECRET OF DIVINE HEALTH....... P   1.25 _____

_____ HOW YOU CAN BE HEALED .... P   1.25 _____

_____ THE REAL REASON WHY CHRISTIANS
ARE SICK .... P   2.50 _____

_____ THIRTY BIBLE REASONS WHY CHRIST
HEALS TODAY .... P   1.25 _____

_____ TWENTY-FIVE OBJECTIONS TO DIVINE HEALING
AND THE BIBLE ANSWERS .... P   1.00 _____

_____ WHY DO THE RIGHTEOUS SUFFER?............ P   1.50 _____

_____ WHY SOME ARE NOT HEALED.................. P   1.25 _____

_____ DIFFICULT QUESTIONS ON DIVINE
HEALING ANSWERED........................... P   1.25 _____

_____ SET OF ABOVE SERIES (10 TITLES) .... P   11.00 _____

MacMillen, S. I.
_____ NONE OF THESE DISEASES..................... P   2.50 _____

(Save $5.00 — Entire Set of Above Books and Tapes ONLY $27.00)

...ABOUT GROWING (IN SPIRIT AND IN FAITH)

Banks, Bill
_____ ALIVE AGAIN! .... P   3.95 _____

Brant, Roxanne
_____ MINISTERING TO THE LORD.................... P   3.95 _____

_____ GROWING POWER OF FAITH .... P   3.50 _____

Billheimer, Paul
_____ DESTINED FOR THE THRONE .... P   2.95 _____

Buess, Bob
_____ FAVOR THE ROAD TO SUCCESS................. P   1.95 _____

Bush, Wes
_____ HOW TO HEAR GOD SPEAK .... P   1.50 _____

Capps, Charles
_____ THE TONGUE: A CREATIVE FORCE .... P   2.95 _____

Carothers, Merlin
_____ POWER IN PRAISE.............................. P   4.95 _____

Gossett, Don
_____ THERE'S DYNAMITE IN PRAISE .... P   2.50 _____

_____ WHAT YOU SAY IS WHAT YOU GET .... P   2.95 _____

Hagin, Kenneth
_____ HOW TO TURN YOUR FAITH LOOSE .... P   1.00 _____

_____ WHAT FAITH IS................................ P   1.00 _____

Jones, Russell B.
_____ GOLD FROM GOLGOTHA .... P   1.50 _____

Miller, Basil
_____ GEORGE MUELLER............................. P   2.95 _____

Murray, Andrew
_____ POWER OF THE SPIRIT .... P   3.95 _____

Price, Charles
_____ THE REAL FAITH .... P   4.95 _____

Trumbull, H.C.
_____ THE BLOOD COVENANT .... P   5.95 _____

Whyte, Maxell
_____ THE POWER OF THE BLOOD .... P   2.50 _____

Wigglesworth, Smith
_____ EVER INCREASING FAITH .... P   1.95 _____

_____ FAITH THAT PREVAILS .... P   1.50 _____

(SAVE $9.40 — Entire set of above books ONLY $49.00)

Send your order listing desired titles to the address below. Please enclose your check, payable to IMPACT BOOKS, INC. and include the information indicated. Thank you.
IMPACT BOOKS, INC., 137 W. JEFFERSON, KIRKWOOD, MO. 63122

Today's Date _____

Name _____

Address _____

City _____ State _____ Zip _____

TOTAL QUANTITY ____ **TOTAL ORDER** ____

Missouri Residents add 6% Sales Tax _____

Minimum Postage $1.50 _____

TOTAL AMOUNT ENCLOSED $ _____

Prices subject to change.
Write for our complete catalog of over 800 Christian Books, Cassettes, and Records.

"HELP ME, I'VE ALREADY HAD AN ABORTION!"

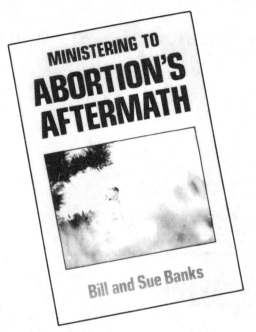

This new book is unique because it offers real help for the suffering women who have already had abortions. This book is full of GOOD NEWS!

It shows how to minister to them, or may be used by the women themselves as it contains simple steps to self-ministry.

Millions of women **have had abortions:** every one of them is a potential candidate for the type of ministry presented in this book. Every minister, every counsellor, every Christian should be familiar with these truths which can set people free.

FOR ADDITIONAL COPIES WRITE:

137 WEST JEFFERSON
KIRKWOOD, MISSOURI 63122